Christ's Glorious Church

The Story of Canterbury Cathedral

DEREK INGRAM HILL

*Regnante in perpetuum Deo et
Domino nostro Jesu Christi*
Anglo-Saxon Charter, A.D. 472

Foreword by
HRH The Prince of Wales

LONDON
SPCK

First published 1976
SPCK
Holy Trinity Church
Marylebone Road
London NW1 4DU

© Derek Ingram Hill 1976

Printed in Great Britain by
Northumberland Press Ltd, Gateshead

ISBN 0 281 02917 2

FOREWORD BY

HRH *The Prince of Wales, K.G., G.C.B.*

It must surely be impossible to visit Canterbury Cathedral without being moved in some way by this spectacular monument to man's ingenuity and artistry. Every time I come here I find something new and even more beautiful which had escaped my notice before. Each time I am filled with wonder at the sheer feat of engineering that was required to create this sculptured masterpiece. Sometimes, as I stand beneath the soaring arches and gigantic pillars, admiring the glory and romance of the whole concept, I forget that it was in fact our ancestors who built the whole thing.

The Cathedral has been part of the life and heritage of this country for so many centuries now, and has weathered so much throughout history that one almost feels it is something exquisitely fashioned by nature alone rather than by man. And yet it was fashioned by men who had a deep understanding of the spirit of nature—of the meaning of stone and glass—and who were bursting to create a physical expression of their spiritual desire to glorify God. In that I believe they succeeded—and probably beyond their wildest dreams. Fourteen hundred years later we are still worshipping and glorifying God within this Cathedral. The very nature of the place is to raise men's eyes and men's minds to greater things; to things of eternity and peace and beauty. To release our souls, albeit briefly from their material imprisonment and to project them into realms of unsurpassed and 'un-earthly' appreciation. That is the wonder and majesty of Canterbury. That is the genius of our forefathers who in many ways understood more about life than we do now. That is why we can always learn so much from a place like Canterbury and that is why it means so much to so many people all over the world. It means a *great* deal to me.

1976   CHARLES

v

Dedicated to Michael and Joan Ramsey
in thankful recollection of
many happy occasions in Canterbury
during the Primacy of the
Hundredth Archbishop

Contents

PLAN OF CANTERBURY CATHEDRAL

SITES OF ANCIENT ALTARS

1 S. Michael
2 S. Gregory
3 S. John the Evangelist
4 SS. Peter and Paul
5 The Holy Trinity
6 S. Thomas of Canterbury
7 Edward the Confessor
8 S. Andrew
9 S. Stephen
10 S. Martin
11 Our Lady
12 S. Alphege
13 S. Dunstan
14 The Holy Cross
15 The Sword's Point

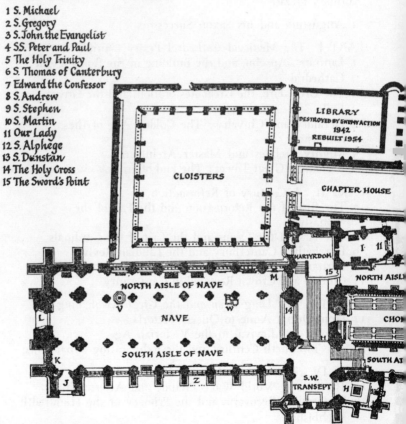

EXPLANATIONS

A Water tower
B Sub vaults
C Treasury (Prior Wibert 1151-1167).
D S. Andrew's Chapel
E Henry IV Chantry
F Corona or Becket's Crown
G S. Anselm's Chapel
H S. Michael's Chapel (Buffs' Memorials)
I The Lady Chapel (Prior Goldstone 1449-1468)
J South porch
K Stairs to parvis

L Western entrance
M Former position of Lady Chapel
N.O.P.Q. Squints from prior's chamber
R Original position of High Altar
S Original position of S. Augustine's Chair
T Site of Archbishop Becket's Shrine
U Present position of S. Augustine's Chair
V Font
W.W Pulpits
X Archbishop's Throne
Y High Altar
Z Site of Chantry Chapel of S. John Baptist subsequently Nevil Chapel
The Angel Steeple completed by Prior Goldstone II (1495-1517)

List of Illustrations

ACKNOWLEDGEMENTS

The grateful thanks of author and publishers are due to Mrs Olive Smith for the use of the six fine photographs of the cathedral taken by her late husband, Mr Edwin Smith; also to the *Kentish Gazette* for permission to publish the photograph of Archbishop Coggan's enthronement, and to Mr Ben May of Lee Russell Ltd of Canterbury for the photograph of an early nineteenth-century print of the cathedral choir, kindly loaned for the purposes of this book by the Canterbury City Museum.

Author's Preface

To write a history of one of the world's most impressive buildings, and one linked for some fourteen centuries with the history of England, might be thought a somewhat daunting and challenging assignment. I only set out on this formidable undertaking in the spring of 1974, when I realized that most of the books about the cathedral of Canterbury which I had read over the last fifty years were out of print and so unobtainable by the ordinary reader; and that to the best of my knowledge no one had yet attempted to write a history of the last fifty years here, exciting and stimulating as they have been, which happen to coincide exactly with my own association with both cathedral and diocese.

The result of two years' hard work, now presented to the general reader, is not intended to be a work of great scholarship or an attempt to provide a successor to the mighty tomes of Somner, Hasted, Dart, or Messrs Woodruff and Danks, but a simple history of the cathedral which may give pleasure as well as information to those who wish to have some account of this great church and those who have built it and made it what it is today after so long a period of time.

Among the many to whom some acknowledgement must be made for help received, I should like to mention the BBC who have allowed me to use some of the material from a series of talks given on Radio Medway in 1973. I owe a considerable debt to Mrs Eve Walber for pruning and shaping my original bulky manuscript; to my friends Canons Robinson and Sargent of Canterbury for much encouragement and advice, as well as to Dr William Urry and Miss Anne Oakley whose massive learning, freely placed at my disposal, has prevented me from making many mistakes and blunders. I am most grateful to Mr John Chesshyre for reading the proofs and correcting some errors in punctuation and the spelling of proper names, and above all to my wife for her patience in living with this work over many months in various stages of preparation and for her help in typing and reading over again and again individual chapters now at last assembled in their final form.

At a time when, as a result of the Cathedral Appeal, there is enormous interest in the famous Mother Church of the Anglican Communion, stimulated by many radio and television features, the appearance of a book like this may be welcomed by new friends of the cathedral as well as older ones. I can only hope that they may come to share my own life-long joy and delight in a splendid building which, to me at any rate, seems to embody in material form something of the majesty and beauty, the glory and loveliness which Christians find expressed supremely in the person of Our Lord and Saviour Jesus Christ, whose name alone our cathedral has borne all through the long centuries of its history.

Canterbury   DEREK INGRAM HILL
The Epiphany 1976

1

Augustine and his Saxon Successors

On a spring day in the year 597, watchers along the Kentish shore might have seen a long-awaited vessel approaching from the coast of France. On board was a company of forty Benedictine monks, who had journeyed from Rome under the leadership of their prior, Augustine. Their long and perilous journey had been undertaken at the command of Pope Gregory the Great (himself a Benedictine monk and the founder of their monastery), who had heard that the Saxon king Ethelbert would welcome Christian missionaries. Ethelbert had married Bertha, a Christian princess from France, and had granted her the right to worship God in a small oratory outside the walls of Canterbury, still surviving as part of the fabric of St Martin's Church.

There had been Christians in Canterbury in late Roman times. According to the Saxon chronicler Eadmer, Augustine found on his arrival a church constructed during this period, perhaps originally a public hall or basilica converted to a Christian place of worship. Nearly two centuries had passed since then, and Christianity was not even a memory. But now there were men to proclaim the faith again, and it was characteristic of Gregory that he should have sent not a mere handful but a whole priory of monks to meet the King's wishes.

Sir Arthur Bryant has said of this mission:

It proved the most important of all the invasions of England and the most peaceful. Marching across the downs from Sandwich with a silver cross and banner under their leader Augustine the monks were received by Ethelbert at his tent door lest they should cast spells on him. He listened to what they had to say, gave them a ruined church in his capital, Canterbury, and resolved to

1

embrace their creed. After he was baptised thousands of his thanes and warriors followed his example.

The baptism of Ethelbert is supposed to have taken place at the ancient font still to be seen in St Martin's Church. Soon after this, Augustine was consecrated bishop and established himself in Canterbury. It seems most likely that he restored and enlarged the ruined Roman church which was on the same piece of ground as the present cathedral and that from the first it was dedicated to Christ Jesus the Saviour. He lived with some of his monks near the cathedral while the rest settled outside the city walls in a monastery dedicated to St Peter and St Paul, later to be known as St Augustine's Abbey.

The first Cathedral Church of Christ in Canterbury seems to have been an imposing building. In an apse at the west end stood the official seat of the archbishop, the cathedra, looking up a long nave with towers on each side. There was a crypt at the east end and over it an aisled choir with an altar approached by a flight of steps. The greatest archbishop of these early centuries was Theodore of Tarsus, a Greek who was sent from Rome with his friend Hadrian who became Abbot of St Augustine's c. A.D. 668. Bede describes the age of Theodore as ideal:

Nor were there ever happier times since the English came into Britain; the minds of all men were bent upon the joys of the Kingdom of which they had just heard, and all who desired to be instructed in sacred reading had masters at hand to teach them. From that time also they began to learn in all the churches of the English a sacred music which till then had only been known in Kent.

From A.D. 682 to 741, the archbishops were buried in St Augustine's Abbey. About A.D. 750 Archbishop Cuthbert added a baptistry at the east end, dedicated to St John Baptist, and in it were buried most of the archbishops from then onwards. Archbishop Odo, a vigorous prelate, had the height of the walls increased and the roof raised (c. 950).

St Dunstan was one of the most celebrated of all the Saxon archbishops. He was not only a great saint and statesman but also an artist and craftsman, smith, bell-founder and even organ-builder, according to legend. In the lower clerestory of the north choir ambulatory are two thirteenth-century windows illustrating stories from his life and miracles. One depicts a vision he had on the Eve of Ascension Day:

The night office of the Cathedral clergy had finished and the Saint was left alone in the church when a multitude of blessed spirits burst in and brought him an invitation from Our Lord to spend the day with them in heaven. He asked some of them who they were and they answered, 'We are cherubim and seraphim.' But Dunstan replied that it was his duty to give the people their communion and preach to them that day, and so declined the offer. (A. J. Mason, *Ancient Glass in Canterbury Cathedral*, p. 46.)

At his death in 998 he was buried in a shrine in the cathedral choir and this became a place of pilgrimage until the end of the Middle Ages.

Since the time of Augustine the cathedral had been staffed at times by monks and at others by secular clergy and the head was known as the Dean.[1]

It was a monk, the saintly Alphege, who was the first archbishop to die a violent death. In 1011 Danish pirates besieged Canterbury, sacked it and burnt the cathedral, and carried off the Archbishop to their camp at Greenwich where they held him to ransom. When the old man refused to allow a levy on his tenants to pay the ransom, he was pelted to death with beef bones at a drunken orgy following a banquet. In 1023, when England was ruled by the Christian Dane, Canute, the body of Alphege was restored to Canterbury and placed in a shrine on the north side of the High Altar opposite the shrine of St Dunstan on the south side. There these two Saxon saints remained until the Reformation swept shrines and relics away.

There is a story of a conversation at a later date between Lanfranc and Anselm. Lanfranc was unwilling to accept Alphege as a martyr because, he said, he did not die for religion but for refusing to ransom his life at the expense of his tenants; the gentle Anselm replied that he was a saint and martyr because he died for righteousness and that he who dies for righteousness dies a martyr for Christ. Lanfranc appears to have been convinced by this argument and the feast of St Alphege has been kept in England on 19 April from those times until the present day.

[1] A title borne by the head of the Cathedral Chapter until the Norman Conquest.

When William the Conqueror landed in 1066, the Saxon cathedral was still intact. But in 1067 it was destroyed by fire. Everything perished, including the crown of King Canute which the King had hung up on the rood in reparation for the murder of St Alphege. The fire coincided with the deposition of the last Saxon archbishop, Stigand, and his replacement by Lanfranc. A new dynasty, a new primate, and a new cathedral all appeared together, and the first great act in the dramatic history of the cathedral really begins at this point.

PART I

*The Medieval Cathedral
Priory Church*

2

Lanfranc, Anselm, and the Building of the Romanesque Cathedral

Archbishop Lanfranc, who was consecrated in a shed beside the ruins of the Saxon cathedral in 1070, was one of the greatest men ever to sit in the Chair of St Augustine. An ardent believer in the monastic life, a great statesman, an efficient organizer, and a man of piety and charity, he stamped the cathedral and monastery of Christ Church with a character that it was never to lose in all the medieval centuries. A cathedral priory was essentially an English foundation in which the bishop was in fact abbot (whether he was a monk or not) and the house was ruled by an elected prior. Lanfranc lived the life of a monk all through his primacy and not only re-built his cathedral church but provided his monks with fine and enduring domestic buildings as well, many of which still survive, though little of his church remains.

The Precentor of the monastery, a Saxon monk called Eadmer, records (*c*. 1100) how Lanfranc had the footings dug out and 'in the space of seven years ... raised this new church from the very foundations and made it nearly perfect'. So far as it can be recon-structed, it seems to have been a typical Norman abbey church built on the pattern of St Etienne, which still survives largely un-altered in Caen. It had a fine west front, a central door leading into a massive nave with triforium and clerestory resting on stout Romanesque columns, at the end of which were transepts and a small sanctuary built over a crypt. The low tower above, surmounted by a figure of the 'Angel of Mighty Counsel' (Isa. 9.6, Vulgate version), was known as the 'Angel Steeple' all through its history. Strangely enough for so great and far-seeing a man, Lanfranc made one grave mistake in building his new church. He made it too small, for soon men began to flock from all parts, perhaps attracted by his

7

teaching and his sanctity. The time came when there were at least a hundred monks and their dependants, the community of monks crowding the stalls provided for them at the east end of the nave. Lanfranc died in 1089 and was ultimately laid to rest in the northeast transept where his name, scratched on the wall of St Martin's Chapel, is his only memorial.

For five years the see was kept deliberately vacant and its revenue appropriated by the evil and grasping King William Rufus. It was not until 1093, when the King thought he was dying, that he appointed as archbishop the reluctant Anselm, disciple of Lanfranc, and an even greater saint and scholar than his master. Much of his time as archbishop was spent in defending the Church against the encroachments of Rufus, who had unfortunately recovered. But he soon saw that his cathedral church must be enlarged and that what was needed for so flourishing a community was a spacious sanctuary. The priors of Christ Church at this period were successively Ernulf and Conrad, men of great ability to whom was entrusted the work of supervising this great extension. The building was begun in 1096 and was virtually completed by the time Anselm died in 1109.

The completed east end must have been one of the finest of its kind in Europe. We can only admire the skill of carvers who worked with axes in creating designs as fantastic as those which adorn the capitals of the west crypt. This undercroft was a complete church under the main sanctuary, with nave and aisles, and processional aisles on each side. On the north and south of the crypt transepts were chapels dedicated to St Mary Magdalene and St Nicholas, and to St Audoen and St Paulinus. Farther east were chapels dedicated to the Holy Innocents and to St Gabriel. In St Gabriel's Chapel are a finely carved Romanesque pillar and mural paintings showing Our Lord in glory among the Angels of the Seven Churches of Revelation, and scenes in which the Archangel Gabriel appears in Scripture. Traces of the central door into the crypt can still be seen in the west wall (which seems to be made largely of rubble from the Saxon church). There is a fine Norman door with a zigzag pattern leading from the Martyrdom transept down to the crypt, and the passage linking it to the transept is also of Norman work with a curious diaper pattern.

The most striking feature of the work of the Norman period is the remarkable series of pillars in the west crypt. The carving was probably done in the first three decades of the twelfth century, though one capital carved with a fluted motif may date from Lanfranc's church. The absence of any special Christian themes of decoration in the carving of this period brought down upon the Benedictine Order the wrath of the austere Cistercian St Bernard of Clairvaux. Certainly the nightmarish beasts and monsters, the jugglers and dancing creatures with musical instruments seem to be of oriental origin and perhaps show the influence of the Crusades, or of commercial links with the Middle East.

Outside the building are other features dating from this twelfth-century addition: the band of interlacing arches running below the lowest range of windows, and also above the windows of the side chapels of St Andrew and St Anselm; the two little towers of St Andrew and St Anselm, each rich with decoration and with a small cap spire on top; and on the north side the Norman treasury attached to St Andrew's Chapel.

Adjoining the treasury, with medieval iron bars still attached to the windows, are the remains of Lanfranc's large infirmary, and some yards to the west of it the charming water tower erected by Wibert, prior from 1151 to 1167. It was he who had supplies of water brought from the hills outside the city, and the conduit house still exists as well as the original pipes which continue to carry water under the precincts wall as they have done for eight centuries. In pre-Reformation times the pipes went up through the central column into the water tower to fill a large basin made of brass and here the monks would pause on their way from the adjacent dormitory at midnight to wash before singing mattins.

The Norman cathedral and its priory must have been one of the most imposing foundations in England. The master mason in charge of the building works was Blitherus, a Saxon, described in a contemporary document as 'the very distinguished master of the craftsmen and director of the beautiful church'. St Anselm did not live to see this magnificent church consecrated and, in all probability, neither did Blitherus. Anselm died in 1109 and was buried in the chord of the apse of the chapel of St Peter and St Paul, later named St Anselm's Chapel. His bones, placed in a copper shrine, became an object of veneration to pilgrims, although his canonization did not take place for more than 300 years.

The official consecration of the church took place on 4 May 1130. King David of Scotland as well as King Henry I of England were present on this great occasion. Gervase, the chronicler monk who described the ceremony, says that the archbishop, William de Corbeuil, performed it 'with all respect and liberality'; and he added that 'so famous a dedication has never been heard of on the earth since the consecration of the temple of Solomon'. In this magnificent church Archbishop Theobald crowned King Stephen and Queen Matilda on Christmas Day 1142. He had succeeded William de Corbeuil in 1139, and it was in his household that a young man called Thomas Becket was trained for the great offices that were to come to him.

The school of craftsmen in Canterbury at that time, attached to the great Benedictine houses, was quite outstanding. They were capable not only of carving work like that in the west crypt, but also of executing the elaborate, illuminated manuscripts that can still be seen in the Cathedral Library, or the wall painting of St Paul shaking off the viper in Malta (Acts 28. 1–6) still visible high upon the north wall of the apse in St Anselm's Chapel.

When Theobald died in 1162 he was succeeded by Thomas Becket, whose career and martyrdom were to make Canterbury world-famous, and transform an impressive, Romanesque monastic church into one of the most fascinating cathedrals of Christendom. Few who enter the corner of the cathedral known as the Place of the Martyrdom can fail to be impressed by what happened there over eight centuries ago. A contemporary chronicle describes Becket's last moments in the dark cathedral, that winter evening of 29 December 1170 :

The Archbishop covered his eyes with his joined hands, bent his neck and said, 'I commend my cause and the cause of the Church to God, St Denys the Martyr of France, to St Alphege and the Saints of the Church.' At the third blow he sank on his knees, his arms falling, but his hands still joined as if in prayer. With his face turned towards the altar of St Benedict he murmured in a low voice, 'For the Name of Jesus and the defence of the Church I am willing to die.' Without moving hand or foot he fell flat on his face as he spoke, in front of the corner wall of the chapel and with such dignity that his mantle which extended from head to foot was not disarranged. As the murderers left the Cathedral a great storm of thunder and rain burst over Canterbury and the night fell in thick darkness upon the scene of this dreadful deed.

To prevent the murderers from desecrating the corpse, it was interred the next day in the undercroft of the cathedral behind the altar of Our Lady, in a stout marble tomb. For the next half-century multitudes of pilgrims came there, many of them to be cured of diseases. On 12 July 1174 the most illustrious pilgrim of the century, King Henry II, came to kneel at Becket's tomb and received a severe scourging from the monks of Christ Church Priory as a public penance for the murder of his former friend.

3

The Great Fire, the Great Restoration, and the Great Exile

The new era of pilgrimage and the canonization of St Thomas the Martyr began with a disaster which was to prove a blessing in disguise. At 9 a.m. on Thursday, 5 September 1174, following the penance of King Henry, fire broke out in a workshop near the cathedral. Sparks and cinders were carried by the wind on to the roof which was made of wood covered with lead. Some six hours later the roof of the choir was suddenly seen to be on fire. One of the horrified monks who saw it was Gervase who wrote an enthralling account of the fire and its aftermath. The whole scene comes vividly to life: the monks and townsfolk, armed with buckets, rushing up ladders on to the roof while the flames fanned by the wind took increasing hold on the building. The monks' wooden stalls caught fire as the burning timbers fell on them and the fire-fighters on the roof were driven off by the intense heat. 'In this conflagration that wonderful and glorious choir made a wonderful and awful appearance. The flames ascended up to a great height and the pillars of the church were damaged or destroyed.'

So perished after less than a century practically the whole choir, leaving behind only shattered arcades, gaping window embrasures, the two Norman towers and chapels of St Anselm and St Andrew, the undercroft of Our Lady, and the great Romanesque nave. Architects were invited to submit designs for the rebuilding of the choir, and we may be thankful that the monks chose the French master mason William of Sens. His great creation, which is one of Canterbury's glories today, was the first important piece of early Gothic architecture to be seen in England. Set firmly on the foundation of the Romanesque crypt, it rises as something fresh and new out of the Norman arcading of the ambulatories, retaining the lovely

12

Romanesque towers of St Anselm and St Andrew as well as their two chapels.

While keeping what he could of the ruined choir, William used new techniques and methods no doubt learnt in Sens itself where the cathedral had just been rebuilt. A possible clue as to how he introduced the monks to some of his ideas can be found in the easternmost bay of that part of the south ambulatory of the choir, which links east and west transepts. Into the upper part of one of the Romanesque semi-circular arches a pointed arch has been carved, with carefully chiselled dog-tooth work like that in the adjoining transepts. It is not difficult to imagine William demonstrating, with the aid of a skilled carver, what the arcades in his new church would look like.

According to Gervase, a year was spent in clearing away the ruins and debris. From the end of 1175 to 1178 the work went on with great speed, pillars being erected and vaults placed in position, the triforia and clerestory above gradually taking shape. The Easter cross arms or transepts were begun in 1178, and then occurred the accident which ended the career of the great French master mason (described in Dorothy Sayers' play, *The Zeal of Thine House*). The 50-ft high scaffolding on which he was standing collapsed and he was thrown to the ground. He was severely injured and rendered incapable of continuing to supervise the work. Before he fell he had been superintending the construction of the great arch of the crossing, and in the centre of it now can be seen a boss showing the paschal lamb and flag. As a quasi-heraldic symbol of the Resurrection of Christ from whom the cathedral derives its name, it might be thought to be a worthy memorial to this great architect, since it was here that his work virtually ended. He returned to France and died two years later.

By great good fortune, however, there was on his staff an Englishman, also named William, capable not only of superintending the rebuilding of the rest of the choir, but of improving on the work of his master. John Harvey, in his book *English Mediaeval Architects*, says that it is to him rather than to William of Sens that the credit is due for the principal stylistic innovations at Canterbury, for the Trinity Chapel and the Corona built after 1178 are far more advanced than the choir.

By Easter Eve 1180, William and his workmen had finished the east transepts and the presbytery, and an altar was set up there with

13

the shrine of St Alphege on the north and that of St Dunstan on the south, and a temporary wall behind. The monks came in solemn procession with Becket's successor, Archbishop Richard. The great paschal candle was lit and the Blessed Sacrament was placed in a hanging pyx over the High Altar which the Archbishop blessed. With bells ringing and the Te Deum resounding through the church, the monastery took possession again of its choir.

The marvellous series of windows which are Canterbury's peculiar glory now began to appear. No doubt the unique didactic scheme was worked out by the monks themselves, and it is more than likely that William of Sens brought with him glaziers from France. As early as 1178 the great figures of the Genealogy of Our Lord, eighty-eight in all, must have been going into the high windows of the choir clerestory. Since nothing comparable to this series appears to exist elsewhere, one wonders why it was chosen. The explanation may be that, according to the Benedictine Liturgy, it was customary to chant the Genealogy of Our Lord according to St Matthew at the end of Christmas mattins and immediately before Midnight Mass, a ceremony performed on Christmas Eve 1170 by St Thomas himself. The St Luke Genealogy was sung at the end of mattins of the Epiphany, and the Canterbury series is made up almost entirely from this, beginning with Adam and ending with a series of roundels showing principal events in the life of Christ in the central windows of the apse. (This series is now largely dispersed into the west and south-west windows of the nave and most of the figures still in the choir clerestory are nineteenth-century copies using some original border and iron work.)

When the ambulatories and transepts were completed, twelve Bible windows were inserted. Three remain showing scenes from the New Testament in the centre, framed between parallels from the Old Testament. When the chapels were completed on the north side of the transepts (St Martin and St Stephen) and on the south side (St John the Evangelist and St Gregory), glass illustrating scenes from the lives of these saints was set up in the east window of each chapel. Only one restored medallion, showing St Martin dividing his cloak with the beggar, survives of these four windows. In the small windows of the North choir ambulatory can still be seen medallions depicting events from the lives of St Dunstan and St Alphege.

Meanwhile, carvers were at work on the great columns of choir and presbytery, and bosses carved to represent foliage were placed in

14

the centre of each compartment of the vaulting. William of Sens used shafts of Purbeck marble profusely, and this provides a charming effect against the massive stone columns which are alternately octagonal and cylindrical. To incorporate the Romanesque chapels of St Andrew and St Anselm, the presbytery and its ambulatories were constructed with a distinct curve at the east end, where the chapels could be linked with the processional path. The roof was raised some 14 ft higher than the old church, and everywhere the pointed arch begins to appear. The Gothic era had really begun.

English William built the east crypt and a chapel dedicated to the Blessed Trinity above, and then added the lovely and unique circular termination of the whole church known as the Corona. It is so called because in the upper chapel the relic of St Thomas's head (a portion of his skull severed in the murder) was preserved in a silver reliquary for pilgrims to venerate. Although it was never completed, it is one of the most singular and beautiful terminations of any Gothic building in existence. The lower storey in the crypt has a floor of ancient encaustic tiles, thirteenth-century glass in the east window, and a vault powdered with the initials I crowned for Our Lord Jesus and M for Mary his mother.

Ten years after the great fire of 1174 the work was virtually finished. By the time Archbishop Richard died in 1184 the Martyr's tomb in the middle of the east crypt was the focus of devotion for innumerable pilgrims. They were watched continually by the monks from their vantage points under the High Altar, in the remarkable vaulted room now known as the Wax Chamber. The new archbishop was Baldwin, an austere Cistercian, who was almost immediately engaged in a monumental row with the monks. It began with his attempt to reduce their standard of living, which he regarded as excessively high for a religious community, since it included game, fish, eggs, and other delicacies sent by the tenants of the Christ Church manors to their monks at Christmas and Easter. When this failed he announced that he intended to found a college of seventy secular canons nearby and that the Pope had granted him a licence to do so. The Christ Church monks, however, suspected that this foundation was intended to be an electoral college which would take from them their ancient privilege of electing the archbishop. In the quarrel that ensued, half of Europe was ultimately involved, including the sovereigns of England and France and, of course, successive popes, since it dragged on for six years.

Services in the cathedral were suspended and violence was used by partisans on both sides. The monks were virtually besieged in the effort to break their spirit but the citizens sided with them and food was smuggled in to them. Among those involved to their cost was the nephew of Thomas Becket, one Ralph, a priest who had just been made Master of the newly established Hospital of East-bridge, founded to cater for poor pilgrims to his uncle's tomb. Since he sided with the monks, their enemies flung him into the city gaol and then set it on fire, but he was lucky enough to escape.

One of the few acts of King Richard I worthy of recollection within the short time he spent in England during his reign took place in 1189, when he came to Canterbury with the King of Scotland. He stayed in the priory, attended a service in the cathedral, and appointed the Archbishop of Rouen as mediator. The monks promised obedience to their own archbishop, who in turn abandoned his project. Peace appeared to have returned when it was learnt that Baldwin had merely shifted his ground to Lambeth, where he had acquired an estate opposite the Palace of Westminster, to which all the materials for his college buildings were being transferred. Then somewhat dramatically he appealed to Rome, and laying aside his office went off to the Holy Land on crusade, with a pilgrim's wallet and staff, in the train of Richard Coeur de Lion. He died at Acre.

The next archbishop, Hubert Walter, must be ranked among the most powerful of medieval prelates. He had gone on crusade as Bishop of Salisbury, and when Richard fell ill it was he who arranged with Saladin a three-year truce which conceded to the Christians in Jerusalem the right to celebrate divine service in the Church of the Holy Sepulchre. When Richard was captured on his way home, Hubert Walter became his viceregent and raised the money necessary to ransom him. He was elected archbishop in 1193, and on the death of Richard Coeur de Lion he crowned King John and received him on a state visit to Canterbury in 1201. In his relations with the Canterbury monks, however, he had to accept defeat. When he attempted to build the college at Lambeth which Baldwin had planned, all their old suspicions were aroused, and in 1198 they secured a mandate from the Pope ordering him to abandon the scheme and to raze the collegiate church at Lambeth to the ground. The manor, however, has remained the London residence of the primates until the present day.

After this, Hubert Walter's relations with his monastic Chapter seem to have been very cordial, and when he died in 1205 he was buried in the Trinity Chapel, in what is not only the oldest surviving tomb but one of the most impressive in the cathedral. On the rooflike top over it four heads are sculptured on the front and one on each side. Two heads are mitred, and all are carved out of Purbeck marble. For many years it was thought to be the tomb of Archbishop Theobald, Becket's patron and predecessor, and in 1890 the Dean and Chapter had it opened. The body of Hubert Walter was found vested in full pontificals with a simple wooden crosier, mitre, chalice, and paten. These have been preserved, some in the Library, and are among the most valuable and interesting medieval relics that the cathedral possesses.

The royal nominee, John de Gray, Bishop of Norwich, was elected with the compliance of the monks and the bishops of the province of Canterbury and promptly enthroned. To secure papal approval King John sent a deputation of monks off to Rome, paying their travelling expenses and furnishing them with the huge sum of 11,000 marks, to secure the support of pope and curia. All this was in vain. Innocent III, one of the most masterful men ever to sit in the Chair of St Peter, had resolved to appoint his friend Stephen Langton, an English cardinal at the papal court. When John discovered that the Pope had secured the support of the monks, he indulged in a burst of typical Angevin rage. The whole community was exiled, and found refuge in the French city of St Omer. Daily services and masses in the cathedral were maintained by the monks of St Augustine's Abbey.

The exile continued for six years. At last the interdict which the Pope had imposed on England, and the growing discontent of John's subjects, had their effect. The King submitted, guaranteed the monks their privilege of free election, and allowed them to return. On 15 June 1213 the life of the monastery and its church began again, and in due course Stephen Langton was enthroned.

He may well be remembered as among the greatest of the archbishops. A scholar who is credited with dividing the Bible into chapters, and a poet thought to have written the Golden Sequence 'Veni Sancte Spiritus', he was also a spiritual leader and statesman. He brought John to the moment at Runnymede when he sealed the Great Charter, with its resounding opening clause 'that the Church of England be free'. In the history of the cathedral his claim to fame is his devotion to the memory of St Thomas. He planned and organized the translation of the Martyr's remains from the tomb in the east crypt to the far more splendid site in the centre of the Trinity Chapel.

The lovely chapel, bare of tombs as yet except for that of Hubert Walter, was now enriched with the series of windows showing scenes from the life of the saint and miracles wrought at his tomb in the crypt. In addition to the beautiful pink marble pillars of the arcade, Archbishop Langton had a handsome mosaic pavement of Cosmati work laid behind the marble chair. This noble seat of Petworth marble, misleadingly known today as 'St Augustine's Chair', then stood at the top of the steps leading from the sanctuary to the Trinity Chapel. The High Altar, with the Blessed Sacrament suspended above it in a pyx, was on the platform below. So the monks in the choir, as they looked east, would see altar, chair, and shrine rising one behind the other.

A curious set of roundels showing the months of the year, the signs of the zodiac, and virtues and vices, which flank the mosaic pavement on each side may have been brought back by the monks from their exile in St Omer. A crescent made of gilded wood, set high up in the vaulted roof over the shrine, is thought to have been brought back from the crusades as an offering to St Thomas, patron saint of many of the crusaders. The shrine itself is known to have been the work of two craftsmen, Walter of Colchester and Elias de Dereham.[1] The lower part was made of stone on arches under which the pilgrims could creep, and on this rested the actual shrine. The body of the saint reposed inside an iron chest, enclosed in a wooden coffin plated with gold and set with many precious stones. The jewels were the gifts of kings, princes, and pilgrims, and the most famous of them was Louis VII's great ruby, the Régale of France.

The shrine was normally concealed under a canopy of wood painted with sacred pictures, and this was raised from time to time with great dramatic effect by one of the monks. On great occasions the prior himself seems to have shown off these treasures, indicating them with a white wand. Pilgrims would also visit the Corona, the empty tomb of the crypt, and, of course, the Place of the Martyrdom in which was erected the 'Altar of the Sword's Point'. On it, in a special case, lay the point of the sword which had administered the

[1] Walter of Colchester was monk-sacrist of St Alban's Abbey and Elias de Dereham was Canon of Sarum.

coup de grâce. (A fifteenth-century representation of that altar is carved over the south-west porch.)

The translation took place on 7 July 1220, in the jubilee year of the saint's martyrdom. Archbishop Stephen took pains to ensure that the ceremony was the most magnificent event in the medieval history of the cathedral. The young King Henry III led the procession from crypt to retrochoir, followed by the four bearers of the shrine, the Archbishop himself, the Archbishop of Rheims, Hubert de Burgh the Justiciar, Randulph the Papal Legate, almost all the bishops and abbots of the realm, and a great train of barons and notables. After the ceremony a splendid entertainment was provided in the Palace beside the west front, while the pipes and conduits of the city are said to have run with wine instead of water, supplied at the expense of the Archbishop from the four wine vaults of the city.

It is also said that the Archbishop provided hay and oats for the horses of the pilgrims all along the road from London to Canterbury. Certainly this great occasion crippled him and his successors financially for years to come. However, he succeeded in drawing the eyes of all Christendom to his superb cathedral and to the great treasure enshrined in it. For the next three centuries pilgrims came to Canterbury from every corner of England and from the rest of Europe as well. The Christ Church community acted as hosts to half the world, and while they continued each day to chant the office and celebrate the Holy Eucharist with great dignity and liturgical solemnity, their church grew in splendour as the offerings of multitudes of pilgrims and gifts of land and money provided them with enormous resources to be used for the glory of God.

4

Heraldry and Chivalry: The Golden Age of the Monastery

The funeral of Archbishop Stephen Langton in 1228 marked the beginning of a remarkable period in the history of the cathedral which only ended with the funeral of the Black Prince in 1376. This era saw the last of the sainted archbishops, Edmund Rich of Abingdon, whose struggles with Henry III led to his exile and death in France. It also saw the rise of the mendicant Orders, the establishment of Franciscan and Dominican houses in Canterbury, the election of a Dominican archbishop, Robert Kilwardby, and a Franciscan, John Peckham. During this period the Black Death was to change the face of medieval Europe, and of the Church. The development of heraldry was to bring colour and richness to the cathedral. The monastery was at the height of its influence and prosperity under Henry of Eastry, Prior from 1285 to 1331.

Eastry's priorate saw the erection of the parclose screen round the choir which is one of the most conspicuous features of the interior of the cathdral. The original door leading into the choir is still there, though concealed like the screen itself by the stone screen or pulpitum erected later. The door leading into the presbytery from the north-east transept remains also from Eastry's day. The screen originally ran right round the presbytery, but the tombs of the archbishops gradually took its place.

The stalls for the monks were set up on both sides of the choir, with seats for 140, arranged in double rows of thirty-five. Unlike those of many of the great monastic churches, the stalls were not equipped with elaborate canopies. This may be the reason for the beautiful carved cresting on the screen; there was a painted dado below, covered with splendid tapestries in Tudor times.

During the forty-six years of his priorate, Eastry cleared the

3 Christchurch Gate (1507–17) adorned with contemporary coats of arms

4 Nave west to east

heavy debt which he had taken on when elected. During his long term of office he spent vast sums of money, perhaps £1 million in modern reckoning, on additions and improvements to the monastic buildings. These included the brewery, which still survives on the north side of the Green Court, the almonry chapel of St Thomas of Canterbury, which survived until 1859, and the chequer building (recently reconstructed as a library after having been destroyed in 1868). As well as adding many books to the monastic library, Eastry was also responsible for rebuilding the chapter house. The lower part, with its great seat for the prior, and stalls at the east end and round the north and south walls, still survives from his day, though the roof and windows were remodelled later.

In view of his great services to the cathedral and to the community, it was fitting that of all the priors Eastry alone should rest in a great tomb. It is in the south choir ambulatory, and a large stone effigy shows him in the pontifical vestments which the Pope had granted as a privilege to the priors of Christ Church. They had the right to wear mitre, ring, and gloves like a bishop on certain occasions in the year, and to carry a crosier; while as peers of the realm they had a seat in the House of Lords.

The tombs of the archbishops had begun to enrich the cathedral since Hubert Walter's day. A notable one of this period is that of John Peckham the Franciscan who died in 1292. This lovely piece of Decorated Gothic work is near the door leading from the Place of the Martyrdom to the cloister. The oak effigy has lost its mitre, but an ogee canopy and a vine motif are part of its charm as well as thirteen carved figures of mitred ecclesiastics who may represent the bishops of the southern province. 'Friar John' is still remembered as the founder of a college of priests in the nearby village of Wingham, though the foundation has long since vanished.

In 1295 Robert Winchelsey was enthroned in the presence of Edward I and his son, the future Edward II. Though there was a close relationship between Church and Crown at this period, Winchelsey spent much of his time opposing the harsh rule of these Plantagenet kings. For this reason perhaps he became popular with the people who venerated him as a saint and made pilgrimages to his tomb (which was destroyed at the Reformation). He was succeeded in 1313 by Walter Reynolds who had been tutor to Edward II. Reynolds deserted the King, however, when Queen Isabella and Mortimer forced Edward's abdication and brought about his death.

Reynolds was probably buried in the tomb next to that of Prior Eastry.

Simon Mepham, who succeeded him, died after only five troubled years as archbishop, and his tomb is the centre of a great ensemble of fourteenth-century art. At the entrance to St Anselm's Chapel, the archbishop lies in a marble sarcophagus inserted in a lovely stone screen with a vaulted roof over the tomb. The screen is carved with little figures of the Evangelists and other saints. On each side of the chapel are wrought-iron gates made in the iron furnaces of Mayfield in Sussex; Mepham had died in his palace there in 1333. Three years later, a Decorated window was inserted in the south wall of the chapel to give more light. This cost £42, and both the tomb and window may have been the work of one Thomas of Canterbury, who probably also designed the great parclose screen round the choir.

Archbishop John Stratford, the next primate, was the first of a new kind of archbishop. From now on they were statesmen and administrators and often canon lawyers, whose services to the papacy won them cardinals' hats. They were often Chancellors of England and lived like great secular princes. They sometimes incurred much popular hatred, and certainly little of the love and enthusiasm that Becket aroused in his role of champion of the people against the Crown. With them came to an end the great medieval period of faith and ardour.

Stratford's tomb in the south ambulatory is a fine piece of work, with a pinnacled canopy over the alabaster effigy of the primate in pontificals, and it bears some resemblance to the contemporary tomb of King Edward II in Gloucester Cathedral. His native town was Stratford-upon-Avon, where he founded the collegiate church of Holy Trinity, and it seems strange that he should not have chosen to be buried there. In 1905 the tomb, which had fallen into disrepair, was restored at the expense of Archbishop Randall Davidson, who oddly enough was the first Bishop of Winchester to be translated to Canterbury since the time of Stratford nearly six centuries before.

Neither of Stratford's immediate successors, John Ufford and Thomas Bradwardine, was enthroned. Both died of the Black Death. It not only killed two archbishops in a matter of weeks, but wrought havoc among the clergy throughout the country, at least one third of whom are thought to have died. (Five rectors were appointed to St Alphege Church near the cathedral in the course of the one year 1351.) Many monastic communities were wiped out altogether but at Christ Church Priory only four monks died at the height of the plague. This suggests that the sanitary conditions were superior to those in other religious houses. The horror and fear which the plague aroused may well have stimulated devotion at the shrine of St Thomas, and in 1350 £800, a vast sum of money in those days, was taken in offerings at the shrine.

The Prior at this time was Robert Hathbrand, another Henry of Eastry, who presided over the fortunes of the monastery for more than thirty years. He seems to have been tutor to Edward the Black Prince, whose devotion to the cathedral perhaps dates back to his boyhood. The Prince's first visit was with his parents in 1331, when he was three years old, and the Prior gave him an alabaster cup. The Hundred Years War broke out five years later, and in 1345 Prince Edward won his spurs at the battle of Crécy. After the victory he adopted the arms of peace, the three ostrich feathers with the motto *Ich dien*, which he is said to have taken from the arms of the king of Bohemia who died in the battle. In time of war he used the Plantagenet coat of arms of France and England quarterly with the motto *Houmont* (High Spirit). After another great victory at Poitiers in 1356, the Black Prince passed through Canterbury on his way home, with his prisoner King John the Good of France, and both made their devotions and offerings at the shrine of St Thomas.

He married his cousin Joan, known as the Fair Maid of Kent, by papal dispensation, and in return founded a chantry in the crypt with two altars maintained by two chantry priests. Each day they said Mass at the altars of the Holy Trinity and Our Lady, and said the Canonical Hours together at the altar of the Trinity. The Prince endowed his foundation with the manor of Vauxhall in London. It belonged to the Cathedral Foundation until the last century, when it was taken over with many other estates by the Ecclesiastical Commissioners. The priests lived together in a house in the parish of St Alphege, and the site is marked by a modern house called the Black Prince's Chantry.

The transformation of the Norman apsidal chapels to form the chantry chapel is one of the most remarkable architectural features of the cathedral. The Romanesque 'body' is clothed with what can only be called a Perpendicular 'robe'. The beautiful stone vault is adorned with richly carved bosses, once gilded and coloured. One shows a pelican in her piety feeding her young with her own blood, and another depicts Samson smiting his enemies with the jawbone of an ass (perhaps an allusion to the Prince's overwhelming victory against superior forces at Poitiers). The most interesting boss is that of a female head in an elaborate head-dress at the west end of the chapel; it is supposed to be that of Princess Joan.

The Black Prince died on Trinity Sunday, 8 June 1376; and the following Michaelmas, after a long period of lying in state in Westminster Hall, his body was brought to Canterbury. He had asked to be buried in the Chapel of Our Lady Undercroft, but the monks thought the only place worthy of so great a lover and benefactor of their community was close by that of the Martyr himself in the Trinity Chapel. Archbishop Simon of Sudbury presided over the funeral ceremonies, singing the pontifical requiem with the assistance of Bishop Courtenay of London and Prior Mongeham. The great company of barons, knights, and heralds present, together with all the members of the Prince's household, must have been apprehensive of the future of a country now ruled by an old man, with a mere boy as heir apparent, at a time of great popular discontent and economic problems produced by the after effects of the Black Death.

After the funeral the coffin was placed in the tomb and a grille, a fine piece of English ironwork, was set round it. Above it hung a massive wooden tester painted with a representation of the Blessed Trinity, to whom the Prince had always felt great devotion. On a beam over all were placed the achievements of arms of the Prince, helmet, crest and chain, jupon, shield and gauntlets, and perhaps his sword and scabbard, though the sword has long since been missing. These may have been the ones worn in battle or tournament, or possibly were made specially for the funeral. Now they lie in a special case at the foot of the Pilgrim Steps, while replicas given by the Friends of the Cathedral in 1954 have taken their place over the tomb.

Heraldry was beginning to be seen as an important element in church decoration. The coats of arms carved on the roof of the Black Prince's chantry are the earliest examples of the use of this art in the cathedral, to be followed by the arms emblazoned on the tomb of the Black Prince. In the time of Prior Hathbrand, the adjoining crypt chapel of Our Lady in the west part of the undercroft was sumptuously adorned with heraldic painting. This lovely chapel was for over a century one of the most splendid and admired

24

corners of the cathedral. Erasmus, visiting it not long before the Reformation, wrote that it was filled with treasures and relics greater than anything he had seen elsewhere. He described it as a royal spectacle far more beautiful than the celebrated shrine of Our Lady of Walsingham. The sanctuary was enclosed with carved stone screens, and protected by a double iron grille, traces of which can still be seen. In the centre of a fine reredos stood a silver statue of Our Lady. The vault was decorated with suns and stars, and the suns had convex silver mirrors inserted in them which must have caught up the light of many candles; and all over the vault were painted coats of arms of benefactors of the priory. Among the forty-nine recorded are those of Henry VI and the Black Prince.

While Prior Hathbrand and his monks were engaged in this work of decoration and alteration within the cathedral, they were also concerned with improvements to the other buildings of the monastery. The great octagonal kitchen has vanished except for a few fragments in the garden of Chillenden Chambers. The beautiful Table Hall of the infirmary, built about 1343, is, however, complete and is now part of the Cathedral Choir House. A chapel was added to the infirmary also at this time, making a lovely Decorated east end to the great Romanesque building. But all that survives is the east window, in a ruined state without tracery, and the north window without its glass. Meanwhile, the old prior was laying plans for a far greater project, and collecting money towards it. At the second centenary of the Martyrdom, in 1370, £44 was given, equivalent to many thousands of pounds in modern money. The momentous decision had been taken to demolish the old Romanesque nave and replace it on the same foundations with something more to the taste of this flamboyant period of the Middle Ages.

5

Mighty Prelates and
Master Architects

Demolition of the old nave began in 1377, and soon only the Norman west towers remained. Both the design and execution of the new building are attributed to Henry Yeveley, the Derbyshire master mason. The Christ Church community was fortunate to be able to employ him, and also to have within its own ranks so able a financier as Dom Thomas Chillenden, their treasurer. He became prior in 1391, and has been described as 'the greatest builder of a Prior that ever was in Christes Churche'.

Yeveley, whose head is carved on a boss in the cloister, must have been a man of great mental power and stature, one of those said to be 'capable of envisaging a building complete and in detail before one stone is laid upon another, and ... of conveying his vision to the actual builders so that they are able to translate it into actual reality'.[1] The reality is still there for all to see, and there are few sights more satisfying anywhere to the lover of great architecture. *The Canterbury Tales* was written at this time, and Chaucer's pilgrims must have watched this great masterpiece gradually rising. (Chaucer himself was then Clerk of the King's Works at Windsor Castle and the Tower of London.) It is not known whether Yeveley saw the nave complete. Documentary evidence shows that after a long period of inactivity things began to move again in the early years of Chillenden's priorate. The windows were glazed and the vault was completed by 1400, the whole work coming to its final completion and beauty by 1405.

One of the men who had longed to see it built had vanished from the scene twenty years before. Archbishop Simon of Sudbury, who

[1] L. F. Salzman, *Building in England down to 1540*, Oxford, Clarendon Press, pp. 4-5.

had donated 3,000 marks towards the project, had foreseen the popular storm breaking. The rebuilding of the city walls and the great west gate with the church of Holy Cross beside it may have been an attempt to turn Canterbury into a well-fortified place of refuge in an evil day. But when that day did come, all was in vain. The Kentish rebels took Canterbury without much trouble, and the old archbishop was caught in the chapel of the Tower of London saying Mass. He was dragged out and butchered with great barbarity while his young king was parleying with Wat Tyler and his men at Smithfield. Some amends for this tragedy were made in Canterbury where he seems to have been well loved. His headless body was laid in a handsome tomb on the south side of the presbytery close to the shrines of St Dunstan and St Alphege, while his head was returned to his native town of Sudbury where it can still be seen, a gruesome relic, in the vestry of St Gregory's Church. A most attractive reminder of his benefactions is the constant appearance of his coat of arms, showing a little white dog on a black ground, in the nave, cloister, and chapter house.

Fortunately for Yeveley and the monks, his successors were equally anxious to see the work completed and lent all the support they could to financing the building. Archbishop Courtenay, a great-grandson of Edward I, persuaded Richard II to donate 1,000 marks. This may explain why the coats of arms of Richard and his two wives appear at the top of the great West window and on the vault at the west end of the nave. In addition, because the demolition of the north wall of the nave had brought down the adjoining cloister walk, Courtenay left £200 in his will in 1396 to build the new south walk of the cloister. This started the remodelling of the whole cloister in the Perpendicular style in place of the more modest Romanesque and early Gothic structure. Courtenay's coat of arms appears in the south walk. He was buried in an alabaster tomb next to the Black Prince. The effigy on top shows him in full pontificals, protected by a typical stout grille of late fourteenth-century iron-work. The marble face suggests an efficient, rather cold-blooded prelate, a persecutor of Wycliffe and his followers.

The next archbishop, Thomas Arundel, was a cousin of the future King Henry IV. He was displaced by order of Richard II the year after his enthronement, in favour of Bishop Roger Walden, and then restored to office by Henry IV after the dethronement of King Richard II. It was in his time that the Great Cloister was so sumptuously built, the architect probably being Stephen Lote, a pupil of Yeveley. He was a Kentish man and a most able architect. Nowhere is the colour and chivalry of Plantagenet times more splendidly in evidence than in the cloister, with its graceful vaulting decorated with more than 800 painted shields. They represent a multitude of donors from kings and emperors down to a monk of Christ Church, Dom John of Sheppey, whose portrait appears in lieu of arms on one of the shields.

The beautiful Decorated door with triple arches leading into the Martyrdom transept was sadly ruined by the Perpendicular vaulting and door thrust into it. The façade of the chapter house, too, was spoilt when this building was remodelled by Lote. However, it bears testimony to his great ability and mastery of his art. He gave it a noble ceiling of gilded and painted Irish oak, a canopied stone seat under a large east window for the prior, seats on each side for the obedientiaries or monk-officers, and, running down each side of this large rectangular building, seats for the rest of the monks. (For their daily chapter meeting, the seniors sat nearer the east end.)

To Lote also is attributed the design of the great pulpitum or stone screen standing at the top of the flight of steps with its rich carvings, at the east end of the nave. This is a splendid piece of work with fine contemporary iron gates leading into the choir. Dr William Urry thinks it was executed by artists in the service of the Court and perhaps paid for out of royal funds. Its most imposing feature is certainly the royal figures on each side of the door which has caused it to be known as the 'Screen of the Six Kings'. These are thought to be Henry V, Richard II, and Ethelbert (carrying a model for the Saxon cathedral) on the left-hand side of the choir door; and Edward the Confessor, Henry IV, and Henry VI on the right-hand side. The figures of Ethelbert and the Confessor are the oldest, set there when the screen was new as a result of a benefaction of Dom Thomas Heerne, one of the monks. (They may have been carved by John Massingham III, a well-known sculptor living in Canterbury c. 1438.) The figure of Henry IV bears a strong resemblance to his effigy on the tomb in the Trinity Chapel where he was buried by Archbishop Arundel, the monks in no way objecting to placing his tomb a few feet away from that of the Black Prince, father of the murdered and supplanted Richard II. In fact throughout the Middle Ages the Christ Church monks skilfully managed to maintain excellent relations with whatever dynasty

28

happened to control the English monarchy, changing sides in the forthcoming Wars of the Roses with remarkable speed and diplomatic finesse. Strange to relate, this fine screen retained both the figures of kings and the lovely frieze of angels when the Puritan onslaught fell on the cathedral in 1643, but the figures of Christ and the twelve apostles vanished then along with 'twelve mytyred saints', leaving the great screen much the poorer for the loss.

Henry IV ended his troubled reign in 1413 at the early age of forty-six. Three months later his embalmed body was brought from London by water and buried in the presence of all his sons. His wife Joan of Navarre survived him by many years and was finally buried with him in 1437. Since Henry chose Canterbury instead of Westminster Abbey, the monks may have hoped that their cathedral would become the mausoleum of the House of Lancaster. If so, they were to be disappointed by Henry V. The tomb of Henry IV is magnificent, with alabaster effigies of king and queen, crowned and robed, on the tomb chest. An iron grille with candle sconces surrounds and protects it (no doubt from the crowds of pilgrims), and hanging over all is a great wooden canopy painted with the coats of arms of England and Navarre, and adorned with many shields and heraldic emblems. At the head and foot of the tomb are wooden panels painted with scenes of the murder of St Thomas and the Assumption of Our Lady respectively. A great work of art like this tomb and that of the Black Prince would have been designed by the best artists of the day working usually in the service of the Crown. Yeveley, therefore, may well have designed the Black Prince's tomb, and Stephen Lote that of King Henry. Modern authorities suggest that the alabaster figures of king and queen may have been the work of Robert Broun, carver of the Savoy, while the great tester is attributed to the royal master carpenter, William Toutmond. The King established a chantry foundation with 'twey priestis to sing and pray for his soul for ever'. To house their altar a delightful little chapel with a lovely fan vault, dedicated to St Edward the Confessor, was erected opposite the tomb in the north ambulatory of the chapel of the Trinity. It is protected by a stout wooden screen, with iron grilles looking into the little sanctuary which had to be built out on slender pillars like stilts into the space behind the infirmary. This elaborate and costly work must have taken a long time to execute as it was not dedicated until 1439, after the death of Queen Joan.

After the victory at Agincourt in 1415, Henry V visited Canterbury. He stayed with the monks at St Augustine's, and attended a solemn Mass of thanksgiving in the cathedral. It was sung by Archbishop Henry Chichele who had just succeeded Arundel and was to be in office for twenty-nine years. This visit may have led to the building of the south-west bell tower, as the shields of arms carved and painted on the vault of its porch include those of many who fought at Agincourt. A new bell tower had been planned ever since the Norman campanile fell in the earthquake of 1382. Now the south-west Norman tower was demolished and a new one built in the fashionable Perpendicular style with the porch below. It was designed by Thomas Mapilton and was original for its time. The lower part was largely the remains of Lanfranc's work, the tower proper being built above this. The bells were moved into it from the Angel Steeple, where they had been housed temporarily, and in 1459 the Bishop of Ross blessed a big bell called 'Dunstan'. This bell, often recast, is now the clock hour-bell, standing under a little shelter on top of the tower, usually called after it.

While the tower was being built, the south-west transept was reconstructed. Margaret Holland, a descendant of Joan Holland, wife of the Black Prince, persuaded the prior to let her rebuild the lower chapel of St Michael which had stood on the east side of the transept since Norman times. Margaret Holland had married first John Beaufort, Earl of Somerset, a son of John of Gaunt, and, after his death, Thomas Plantagenet of Lancaster, Duke of Clarence, one of the royal family. This impetuous duke flung himself and a small force of men against a large body of French soldiers at Beaugé near Angers and was promptly cut to pieces, a disaster which did more to smash the myth of English invincibility in France than anything else. At Margaret Holland's death in 1439 St Michael's Chapel, in the new Perpendicular style, was ready and in due course a superb alabaster tomb with effigies of the duchess lying between her noble husbands was placed in the centre. The architect was probably Richard Beke, at that time in charge of the priory works. The elaborate tomb lies under a vaulted roof, carved and painted with the arms of Holland, Plantagenet, and Beaufort. The alabaster effigies are carved in great detail and are laid on a Purbeck marble base. Even the pins which fasten the duchess's head-dress can be seen and the armour of the two noblemen is accurate in every detail. The jewelled circlet on the head of the Duke of Clarence recalls the story of the fortunate Scottish soldier who was at Beaugé, fighting on the side of the French, and who was able to secure the circlet from the dead man's helm and sell it for a great sum of money.

This chapel has become known as the Warriors' Chapel because of the number of soldiers who were buried there in post-Reformation days. In modern times it has become, appropriately, the Regimental Chapel of the Buffs (East Kent) Regiment.[2] More impressive than the grandiose effigies of these medieval people is the simple coffin, like a stone tomb, in which Stephen Langton was buried in 1228. This had once fitted under the altar into the chord of the apse, but it seems to have been difficult to place in the same position against the new rectangular east end of the chapel. So the curious device was adopted of placing the east extremity of the tomb out in the churchyard, the coffin-tomb sticking through the wall with the west end protruding under the altar. It shows a strange lack of respect for the remains of one of the most illustrious of archbishops.

The chapel above, dedicated to All Saints, is a beautiful room with a vaulted ceiling on which are carved, as bosses, three cowled heads of priors, usually identified with Chillenden, Wodensburgh, and Molash. The chapel was restored to use for devotional purposes in 1950, having been for many years a lumber room. Some of the original Norman work was uncovered during the restoration and can be seen in the west wall, which is pierced with windows looking down into the transept below. The reconstruction of the south-west transept to harmonize with the new nave, and the insertion of the huge south window, seem from the heraldry on the vault to have been carried out between 1440 and 1450. A similar reconstruction of the north transept followed twenty years later, in the reign of Edward IV, whose coat of arms with that of many notable people of his time adorns the vaulting over the Place of the Martyrdom of St Thomas.

[2] Now known as The Queen's Own Buffs the Royal Kent Regiment.

6

Building a Great Tower: The End of an Era

The last century and a half of the monastery was closely interwoven with the personalities of the archbishops, many of whom were made cardinals as a reward for their services to the papacy. An exception was Henry Chichele, whose sturdy patriotism did not endear him to the Pope. He was, however, one of the best archbishops of the period and gave great support to the building projects on hand during his long reign of thirty years. His tomb in the presbytery is one of the most colourful in the cathedral. It is a brilliant 'two-decker' tomb, with the primate lying in full pontificals above and little figures of clerks praying for the repose of his soul, while below is a skeleton in a winding-sheet. This *memento mori* is thought to have been placed there during his lifetime to recall to him the common fate of peasant and prelate alike. He was the founder of All Souls College, Oxford, an act of reparation for the slaughter in the Hundred Years War for which he may well have felt some responsibility as a minister of Henry V. To this day All Souls arranges for the restoration of his tomb every fifty years.

The other splendid tomb, facing it, is that of Archbishop John Kemp. Enthroned in 1452, he died two years later but left behind as a visible memorial a fine parish church and a college of secular priests in his native town of Wye, near Canterbury. His tomb has lost some of its heraldry and adornments but its canopy of painted oak tabernacle-work is one of the finest pieces of medieval woodwork extant.

During this period the monks were at last able to arrange for the glazing of the great west window of the nave. When it was built, about 1400, it had been filled with heraldry and figures in the tracery only. Now twenty-one figures of the kings of England, from Canute to Henry VI, were placed in position. They were certainly the work of a master glazier, perhaps John Prudde the Court glazier, and eight remain today, richly dressed monarchs standing on architectural bases under canopies of pearly white glass.

Christ Church monastery seems to have been exceptionally fortunate in its priors and treasurers in its last century, and Thomas Chillenden's work of making the cathedral ever more magnificent was ably carried on by his successors. Their community was continually called upon to show hospitality to eminent visitors. In 1400 the Eastern Emperor Manuel was in Europe, seeking help from the Christian sovereigns of the West, and he visited Canterbury on his way to London. The Holy Roman Emperor Sigismund enjoyed Christ Church hospitality in 1416, and the coats of arms of both empires were put up on the vault of the new cloister.

Two remarkable visitors later in the century were a Bohemian prince and a future pope. Lev, brother of the Queen of Bohemia, was awestruck at the size of the cathedral, 'as high as three churches on top of one another'. And a young Italian diplomat, later to become Pope Pius II, described the shrine as 'that which obscures the fame of all else, covered with diamonds, pearls, and carbuncles', adding that at Canterbury it was considered a crime to offer any material baser than silver. The monks told their visitors an apocryphal story about Louis VII who gave the great ruby called the Régale of France. They said he had offered 100,000 pieces of gold instead of the great ring, but that the ruby had leaped from his ring of its own accord and adhered miraculously to the gold-plated shrine. The monks maintained that if he were to be captured in battle, the king of England could be ransomed by this one stone alone, if it could be sold.

The rebuilding of the north-west transept and the adjoining Lady Chapel recalls in the heraldry of glass and stone the brief triumph of the House of York, and the colourful reign of Edward IV which was to be followed by disaster for his house and the tragedy of the mysterious death of his young sons, the princes in the Tower. The Church of England was dominated for over thirty years by Thomas Bourchier, a great-grandson of Edward III. He acquired for the see the great house of Knole and there, as in the cathedral, can be seen blazoned his device, the curious Bourchier knot. This appears all over his tomb in the presbytery which was carefully sited and built so as not to obscure the light from the High Altar. (His chantry foundation was attached to the altar of St Stephen in the transept close by.) The tomb has lost much of its statuary and heraldry but retains four charming stone figures of St Katherine of Alexandria depicted as princess, scholar, and martyr, from which we may deduce that she was Bourchier's patron saint.

Bourchier's coat of arms appears again on the vault of the Martyrdom transept amid a rich constellation of Yorkist heraldry, and still more conspicuously in the lovely east window of the Lady Chapel. Five rich coats of arms provide a splash of colour in a window made up of sea-green quarries stamped with the ubiquitous knot. This chapel, which replaced the Norman apsidal chapels dedicated to St Benedict and St Blaise, was built between 1448 and 1455 in the priorate of Thomas Goldstone I and even today, shorn of its carved stalls and rich appointments, it is still one of the loveliest corners of the cathedral.

The greatest achievement of the Yorkist period was the transept window known as the Royal Window, because the glass in it was given by Edward IV to commemorate the marriage of his ancestor Edward I to Margaret of France. That ceremony in 1299 had taken place in accordance with medieval custom, just inside the door leading from cloister to transept, the principal door into the cathedral for the monastic community. The glazing is thought to have been carried out in about 1478 by William Neve, the king's glazier, and the main lights were filled with great figures of Our Lady and St Thomas of Canterbury. These disappeared in 1642, but we can still see a company of saints in the tracery at the top, including prophets, apostles, and prelates among whom are St Anselm, St Dunstan, and St Thomas. The portrait gallery of the royal family shows them at their prayers, in a band of colour running across the window: the two young princes, the king, his queen, Elizabeth Woodville, and the five daughters headed by Princess Elizabeth, the White Rose of York. (Her marriage, solemnized by Cardinal Bourchier in 1485, was to end the Wars of the Roses and set the seal on the triumph of Henry VII and the Tudors.)

With the fall of the House of York on Bosworth Field and the coronation of Henry VII, a new age dawned which marked the end of the Middle Ages, and only half a century or so remained to the monastic Orders in England. A sign of the times was the fall in revenues at the shrine and holy places associated with St Thomas, which shows that men's minds were turning away from pilgrimages and medieval devotion to the saints. But the Christ Church community was still rapt up in grandiose building projects which were stimulated now by three people, the all-powerful Cardinal Archbishop John Morton, the zealous Prior William Sellinge, and a great architect, John Wastell. Their partnership was to give England as well as Canterbury one of its greatest monuments: Bell Harry Tower. This project, long planned, had stuck at the lower stages just above the nave roof fifty years before, and if the tower had been built then it would doubtless have been all of stone. But this was the Tudor age, when brick was being used for palaces like Hampton Court and St James's; and it was decided that the great tower should be built of brick, but cased in stone to match up with the rest of the building.

Cardinal Morton took a great interest in the whole scheme for which nearly half a million bricks were needed. Prior Sellinge wrote to him in about 1494 when the work was just beginning:

Most Reverent Father in God and my singular good Lord ... I have communed with the bearer of this letter, John Wastell, your mason, to perceive of what form and shape he will keep in raising up of the pinnacles of your new tower here. He drew unto us the patterns of them, the one was with double finials without crockets and the other was with crockets and single finials. These two patterns please it your good Grace to cause the said John Wastell to draw and show then unto you and upon the sight of your good Grace shall show him your advice and pleasure which of them two or any other to be devised shall content your good Lordship to be appointed. And further if your good Grace would require the said John Wastell so to do I think that he might so provide that these pinnacles be finished and accomplished the next summer following the which it might be so then your tower outwardely shall appear a perfect work.

It is a pity that Morton, usually remembered as a crafty and intriguing politician who thought up the fiscal device known as Morton's Fork, has not been given the credit for this mighty building. From the profusion of badges and rebus devices carved on the exterior of the tower, and from the presence of his arms and those of his master Henry VII carved on the fan vault which is such a feature of the tower inside, it is clear that he provided a great deal of money for its erection. It seems to have been largely built between 1494 and 1497, and during those years the monk treasurer paid out £1,035

35

per annum on it, including £388 for 1,132 tons of Caen stone. The total bills were equivalent to nearly £1 million in modern values. In this context, John Wastell's salary for his later work on the vault of King's College Chapel, Cambridge, was £13 6s 8d per annum, equal now to £3,000 a year. The great treadmill which he installed to raise the masses of brick and stone for the Bell Harry Tower is still in the upper storey, and was used in 1974 to raise equipment to the summit for a television relay of a Sunday service!

Prior Sellinge died in 1494, so he never saw the tower completed. He gave to the complex of monastic buildings the delightful little gatehouse which bears his name on the Green Court side of the cathedral. In it he placed the fine collection of books and manuscripts he had collected abroad on his official embassies to Rome. His successor, Thomas Goldstone II, was in office when the tower was finished. His rebus, three gold stones on a blue ground, is conspicuous on the great strainer arches at the east end of the nave. These had to be inserted to carry the weight of the tower. It takes its name from the fact that Prior Henry of Eastry gave a bell to be hung in the original central tower a century and a half before, and has nothing to do with Henry VII or Henry VIII.

Cardinal Morton died in 1500 and was buried under a large slab with a huge brass on it, in front of the altar of Our Lady Undercroft. A handsome cenotaph was erected a few feet away, showing him in full pontificals with little clerks in fur almuces kneeling around him in prayer, and with many of his badges adorning the monument. Most of the statues have been mutilated but the painting of the Annunciation which forms a reredos at the east end of the monument has been beautifully reconstructed by Professor E. W. Tristram.

Not content with the building of a splendid tower, the monks went on adorning the cathedral to the very end. The great wall painting showing the legend of St Eustace, or Hubert, patron saint of huntsmen, must have been done about this time. It was placed on the wall at the east end of the north choir aisle, and although it is faded it can be studied in detail with the aid of the series of paintings made by Professor Tristram also. Heraldic glass and small quarries dating from this early Tudor period include the arms of Archbishop Warham and Henry VIII, and the rebus of Thomas Goldwell, the last prior, a golden well with the letters T and G over it which appears in a window in St Anselm's Chapel among other places.

The portrait of the Saxon queen Ediva also dates from this time. It now hangs on the north wall of St Martin's Chapel near the place of her burial. Although little is known about its origin or the artist, the story is told of how Queen Ediva gave the title deeds of eight manors to Christ Church priory in 961, laying them with her own hands on the High Altar. The inscription below the painting records the names of the manors supposedly given by her to the priory. Another late medieval painting, of the Flagellation of Christ, survives only in a fragmentary form, and is hung in the Cathedral Library.

Meanwhile, the death of Prince Arthur and the remarriage of his young wife Catherine to his brother, the future Henry VIII, was to lead to profound changes for the community, though at that time the event left its mark only on the cathedral precincts. The gatehouse on the south-west of the cathedral was almost certainly intended as a memorial to Prince Arthur. On its south face are his arms, and those of Catherine of Aragon, Henry VII, William Warham the reigning Archbishop, and Prior Goldstone II, as well as his friends and members of his household who are thought to have subscribed to its building. The fine red brick Tudor core is concealed, like the Bell Harry Tower, by beautiful stonework carved with some early Renaissance ornament. With its restored heraldry and twin turrets it is an imposing entrance to the precincts, although it lost in 1642 the great statue of Christ in the central niche over the gate.

It is not difficult to imagine the many famous people who have passed through its portals in the last four and a half centuries. Amongst them were Henry VIII and the Emperor Charles V, accompanied by Cardinal Wolsey, Archbishop of York, and William Warham, Archbishop of Canterbury, on Whit Sunday 1520. They were received by Prior Goldwell and his monks, vested in rich copes, and escorted to the shrine. Later during their stay Archbishop Warham gave a great ball at the Palace when Charles V danced with Queen Catherine of Aragon and Henry VIII with Charles's mother. All the great ones present, except the Emperor Charles, were able to look up at the gate and see their coats of arms glittering on the stonework.

It was a splendid occasion, and few can have had any inkling that the Middle Ages were at an end. Although this was a jubilee year 350 years after the Martyrdom, the usual celebrations may not have taken place. Pope Julius II wanted too large a share of the expected offerings to go towards his great project of rebuilding St Peter's in Rome. Perhaps the prior and his monks had heard of a German monk called Martin Luther, who three years before had nailed his famous theses to the door of the University Church of Wittenberg, thereby setting in motion the forces which were to bring about the Reformation of the Church in Europe and sweep into limbo so much of the medieval past including the rich and powerful Benedictine Priory of Christ Church, Canterbury.

One illustrious visitor was to see Canterbury again before the blow fell. George Cavendish, the body servant of Cardinal Wolsey, has left an account of the Cardinal's visit for the Feast of the Translation of St Thomas in 1527. At the solemn procession before pontifical High Mass, the community sang the Litany of the Saints coming up the nave, the Cardinal kneeling at the choir door. As he knelt he was seen by his devoted servant to be weeping very bitterly. It is not known whether he wept for the fate of Rome which had just been sacked by the troops of Charles V, or for his own fall which he may have felt was inevitable, or for the monastery which was to share his fate and pass into oblivion a few years hence.

PART II

A Century of Reformation

7

The Rise of the Reformation and the Fall of the Monastery

The Whit Sunday pilgrimage of 1520 was at once the culmination and farewell to the medieval centuries. It was the zenith of Canterbury's glory, with the great tower crowning the splendid church, its gate brilliant with Tudor heraldry and the church itself rich with marvellous stained glass windows and crammed with chantries, monuments, and the treasures of centuries—tapestries, copes and chasubles, monumental brasses, carved and painted statues, and mural paintings everywhere. In the city outside the walls of the precincts were Dominican and Franciscan monasteries, houses of canons and communities of nuns, amid an equally large number of parish churches, hospitals for the poor and aged, all within the walled city with its great gates and bastion towers, the mighty foundation of St Augustine's Abbey dominating everything on the east side, and the rich Kentish countryside sweeping up to the very edge of the old city.

The years after the Whitsun visit must have been a time of mounting anxiety for the prior and the community as they saw ominous signs of violent change. Long before the destruction of the shrine of St Thomas in 1538, it must have been obvious that the pilgrimages were coming to an end, with a change in religious and social attitudes. Not only were the distinguished and highborn whose visits were recorded, like the Duchesse de Montreuil, Dean Colet, and Erasmus, cynical about the relics, but the stream of ordinary pilgrims was drying up. The meticulous records of the monastic accountants show an all-time record figure of £1,142 received in offerings at the shrine and other holy places in 1220, the year of the translation of St Thomas. Figures were steady, around £545, in Chaucer's time, but dropped as low as £25 in 1444, and finished off

41

at the time of the Dissolution at about £36 per annum. The community, however, relied largely for financial support on their vast holdings in land all over the country, thousands of acres in Kent and also in Surrey, Oxfordshire, Essex, and Suffolk.

The last of the great medieval archbishops, William Warham, died in 1532. When not at Lambeth or Canterbury he had lived in enormous palaces like Otford or Knole, entertaining on a huge scale. His enthronement feast on Passion Sunday 1504 was one of the grandest ever, with 3,000 guests, and innumerable fish dishes since it was Lent. Yet the picture of him by Holbein shows a venerable and scholarly old man, the patron of Erasmus, who had the misfortune of being archbishop when Cardinal Wolsey was trampling on the traditional rights of the see of Canterbury. Warham survived long enough to see his rival humbled and disgraced and finally dead, while he himself was buried in a handsome tomb a few feet away from the site of the Martyrdom. Although much spoiled by eighteenth-century restoration, it is still imposing, with a fine effigy of the old archbishop and much heraldry.

Shortly before his death Warham presided over the meeting of the Convocation of Canterbury which accepted with some reservations the supremacy of the Crown. Early in his primacy Warham is supposed to have said that an archbishop named Thomas would be the ruin of the see of Canterbury as St Thomas had glorified it. Only six months after he died the prophecy was fulfilled with the appointment of his successor Thomas Cranmer. Business of state, namely the pronouncement of the divorce of Henry VIII from Catherine of Aragon, and the marriage and coronation of Anne Boleyn, kept him busy for many months and he was not formally enthroned until 3 December 1533. Then, barefoot, in pontifical vestments, he walked to the cathedral through streets which had been carefully sanded. The enthronement ceremonies were as usual, and the priory produced such numbers of swans and partridges for the great banquet afterwards that it left itself somewhat thinly supplied for Christmas.

The ensuing years were full of trouble and gathering clouds for the monks. The disastrous affair of Elizabeth Barton, the Holy Maid of Kent, led to the execution of two senior members of the community. Dr Bocking was warden of the manors, and Richard Dering cellarer of the priory. Even Archbishop Warham had been involved with this nun who was supposed to see visions and was listened to by many when she began to prophesy doom against the king if he persisted in pressing for a divorce. She was executed with her two associates after being examined by Archbishop Cranmer. He advised the prior and his monks to present the king with £200 in token of their fidelity to him. But no bribes or presents could avert the impending dissolution.

In 1534 Dr Layton was sent as a royal commissioner to examine the monastery and by some strange accident was nearly burnt to death in a mysterious fire which broke out in the great dining chamber. His main interest was not in the moral or spiritual state of the community but in its treasures of jewels, plate, and money, for his first action was to set monks to guard the shrine which he intended to take down, sending all the jewels to the Abbey of St Augustine. However, the shrine survived until 1538 and by that time the dissolution of St Augustine's had been achieved.

In 1534 also, Cranmer presided over the session of Convocation which officially repudiated papal jurisdiction in England. He presided too over the trial of St Thomas of Canterbury. The saint was declared a traitor and orders were given for the destruction of the shrine and the seizure of all the gold and jewels which formed part of it. It is said that some twenty-six cartloads of valuables were loaded up and taken to London. Unfortunately for them the monks had tended in the last two centuries of the Middle Ages to invest money in plate and ornaments rather than in land.

When the end came there was no bloodshed, and no destruction of the cathedral as with the Romanesque Abbey of St Augustine. The monks would have been aware that in monasteries attached to cathedral churches complacent priors had become deans of the new foundations, and their senior monks canons residentiary. In addition, places as minor canons had been given to the young monks, life pensions being paid to those who chose to retire into private life. So even the aged Prior Thomas Goldwell, who had written to Cromwell in 1538 suggesting that he and his brethren would never forsake their religious habit and become secular priests, changed his mind two years later and wrote again, asking for the office of dean on the new foundation. But it had already been promised to a wily diplomat, Dr Nicholas Wotton, so when the commissioners came to receive the surrender of the monastery in 1540, the old prior took his pension of £80 a year (worth several thousands of pounds in modern money). He lived in retirement for fifteen years and continued to receive this annual sum. Other monks also took pensions and retired, but of the fifty-three who were in the monastery at the time of the surrender, twenty-eight stayed on and helped to bridge the gap between the two eras.

44

8

The First of the Deans and the Last of the Cardinals

As far back as 1528 Cardinal Wolsey had sought permission from Rome to create new bishoprics out of dissolved abbeys, using the abbey church as the cathedral, transforming the monastic chapter into one of secular canons, and appointing the abbot or some other suitable person as bishop of the new diocese. A bull of Pope Clement VII in 1529 authorized Cardinal Wolsey and Cardinal Campeggio to do this, but both were removed as a result of Henry VIII's failure to secure a divorce from Catherine of Aragon.

It was Cranmer and Cromwell who put Wolsey's scheme into action. Canterbury was one of the last to undergo this transformation which preserved the cathedral and many of the old monastic buildings as well as ensuring some continuity of liturgical life and general administration. If Cranmer had had his way, something like an Oxford or Cambridge college might have appeared instead of the cathedral chapter which replaced the monastery, but he was overruled, perhaps by the conservatism of King Henry. Canterbury's new foundation consisted of a dean, twelve residentiary canons, twelve minor canons, and a large musical foundation of twelve lay clerks, ten choristers, and a master. There were also twelve bedesmen and the usual retinue of vergers, bell ringers, gate porters, and servants for the common hall. The most interesting feature was the creation of the King's School with fifty scholars, a headmaster, and an usher. This had parallels elsewhere, but special to Canterbury was the creation of a small college of six preachers.

This very large company of people, almost as great as the dissolved monastery, was presumably thought necessary for the dignity of the metropolitan Church. The best testimony to the thought and care put into the preparation of the new statutes is the fact that the cathedral is still served by substantially the same kind of officers, though the twelve residentiary canons have now fallen to four, while the minor canons seldom number more than two. There are usually no more than four bedesmen (no longer appointed by the Crown as they were until the Second World War), but they still grace the cathedral processions, wearing gowns with a Tudor rose on one shoulder, and carrying a white staff. The King's School still has its surpliced scholars and two masters, prominent on all great occasions in the cathedral, though there are now some 900 boys (and girls) and a very large staff.

Most interesting of all is the survival of the little college of six preachers, nearly 200 of whom have held office down to the present day. Their duties, though, have shrunk from regular preaching in the cathedral and in parishes dependent on it, to one sermon a year on a Sunday afternoon in the cathedral. They now have only an annual honorarium in place of their original stipend of £25, a free house, an allowance of firewood, and a horse to get them to their preaching engagements.

In theory the new foundation ought to have worked as well as the old, but the reverse was the case. It is impossible to read the history of the cathedral for the next 300 years without feeling that Cranmer was right and King Henry wrong about the people entrusted with its care. From the start things went wrong at Canterbury and this was due both to the system and to the clergy. Instead of a monastic community of celibate monks totally devoted to their church and its liturgical life, constantly striving to enrich its fabric and ornaments, with a prior to guide and govern them, there was substituted an absentee dean and twelve canons, six of whom had been senior monks in the old community and six of whom were secular priests. Of these canons, two seem hardly or never to have resided and two were nonentities. Among the others were Nicolas Ridley, who became Bishop of Rochester, and Richard Thornden, a former monk and later Bishop of Dover who was to give Cranmer much trouble in Queen Mary's reign. Of the former monks, ten became minor canons, nine (presumably novices) became scholars of the King's School, and two more were made choristers.

An attempt seems to have been made to balance men of a traditional outlook with others more radical who were embracing the Protestant ideas coming from the Continent. The six preachers were equally divided between these two factions. The result was disastrous.

46

Intrigues, plots, and violent sermons attacking the opposite party resounded in the cathedral and parish churches. Things might not have been too bad if the dean had been ready to devote himself to the well-being of the cathedral, but the choice fell on the last man in England capable of making this his life's work.

Nicholas Wotton, appointed dean in 1540, did not even get himself installed until 1542, and two years later he accepted the deanery of York as an additional preferment. For the next twenty-five years he saw as little as possible of either place. He was a professional diplomat much trusted by successive monarchs. The measure of his diplomacy may be gauged by the fact that though he was one of those responsible for the fiasco of Henry VIII's marriage to Anne of Cleves, the King bore him no grudge but left him a legacy and appointed him one of his executors. He continued to serve Edward VI, and having refused several bishoprics out of a sense of unfitness for the office, he finally refused the archbishopric of Canterbury on the deprivation of Cranmer. But though he seems to have been a pleasant and able man of Catholic sympathies, tireless in the diplomatic service of his country, he was a disastrous dean, being frequently non-resident, and as a result his chapter was rent by quarrels and factions.

Waste and plunder of the cathedral treasures and possessions were the order of the day. First there was an interval of nearly a year between the fall of the priory early in 1540 and the establishment of the new foundation in April 1541, when no one seems to have been in charge. Some mystery attaches to this period. Who took the services and by what authority? The old Latin rites remained in use all over England until the introduction of the First English Prayer Book in 1549. One can only suppose, if services were not suspended altogether, that those monks who opted to remain as secular priests must have been responsible. By the time the new chapter was set up some plate had vanished, and when Dean Godwyn took the place of Dr Wotton in 1567 only about one tenth of the ornaments remained. This was in a cathedral which in 1540 had had over 200 copes of varying colours and forty sets of eucharistic vestments.

Dr Wotton set the fashion for deans for the next century to be buried in the cathedral. In the Trinity Chapel, hard by the tomb of Henry IV, his nephew set up one of the most handsome Renaissance monuments in England. It shows the little dean, a dapper, bearded figure in a long surplice and full academic hood, at prayer at a desk with a classical pyramid behind. Over the tomb and on its sides are heraldry showing the deanery of Canterbury and also that of York, the whole enclosed in a fine contemporary wrought-iron railing. He also set a heraldic fashion by impaling his personal coat of arms with those of the dean and chapter originally used by the Benedictine community until 1540 (in heraldic terms: azure, a cross argent with the letter 'x' surmounted by the letter 'l' on the cross).

While Dr Wotton was away on his diplomatic career, the cathedral clergy were busy intriguing and quarrelling among themselves. The priests gathered together represented all shades of the ecclesiastical spectrum. The first six men to be appointed preachers were Lancelot Ridley, a first cousin of the Protestant martyr Bishop Nicolas Ridley; Michael Drume, a canon of Wolsey's Cardinal College at Oxford who had been in prison for his radical opinions; Thomas Brooke, deprived under Mary Tudor for being married; John Scory, an ex-Dominican who became Bishop of Rochester in 1551 but was deprived by Mary for his radicalism; and Robert Searles and Edmund Shether, both strong conservatives who had spent some time in prison for heresy, the former being involved in the celebrated Prebendaries Plot against Cranmer.

The real cause of the dissension at Canterbury and elsewhere was the open Bible which, thanks to the recent invention of printing, now lay close to the hand of every man and woman who could read and interpret as they pleased. In 1538 Henry VIII had ordered a copy of the Bible in English to be placed in every church; and in 1541 a Tudor arch, with a wooden desk underneath on which was chained a copy of the English Bible, was installed in the north ambulatory of the cathedral. The arch and desk are still there, with a copy of a large Bible dating from 1572. After the death of Henry VIII came the changes of the Protestant régime of Edward VI's reign. The Latin service books disappeared overnight at Whitsuntide 1549, in favour of the First English Prayer Book.

The conservative Henry VIII was hardly buried before the pillage of such foundations as had escaped the dissolution of the monasteries was resumed, notably the great number of chantries which had been founded in cathedrals, religious houses, and parish churches. Their suppression, and the confiscation of their revenues and possessions, had been planned in 1545 but it was not until 1547 that an Act of Parliament placed these institutions, some 2,374 in all, at the disposal of the Crown. Originally this suppression had been intended to finance the wars against France and Scotland. In fact, as with the dissolution of the monasteries, it was an excuse for pillage by Crown and nobility, the equivalent of many millions of pounds in modern money being realized by the sale of lands, plate, vestments, and property. A manuscript in the cathedral library records that among the chantries dissolved were those of the Black Prince, Bishop Buckingham, Archbishop Arundel, Dame Joan Brenchley, Cardinal Beaufort, Cardinal Bourchier, and Archbishop Warham. Henry IV's chantry seems to have been dissolved before this, probably in 1540 at the time of the dissolution of the priory.

The years of pillage and liturgical change that followed the death of Henry VIII were suddenly followed by the death of Edward VI and the great reaction after the accession of Mary Tudor. The first victims were Cranmer himself and his brother Edmund, Archdeacon of Canterbury and a residentiary canon since 1534. Cranmer was imprisoned, and his brother fled to Germany. Several of the canons were also deprived, usually for being married men, and replaced by loyal supporters of the old ways, among them Nicholas Harpsfield. He was made canon and archdeacon of Canterbury early in Mary's reign and seems to have been a diligent hunter out of heretics. Nearly all the six preachers were deprived either as being married or for heresy and one of them, Rowland Taylor, who had been Cranmer's chaplain, was burnt for heresy in his own parish of Hadleigh in Suffolk.

Dr Wotton was, of course, out of England, on an embassy so the conduct of affairs in the cathedral was in the hands of Richard Thornden, the Vice-Dean, an ex-monk who promptly restored the Latin rite and its accompaniments without Cranmer's knowledge or authority despite the fact that, at the Archbishop's recommendation, he had been consecrated suffragan bishop of Dover in 1544, holding this office with his canonry. Since rumours were going round that Cranmer was responsible for the restoration of the Latin Mass in Canterbury and elsewhere, the Archbishop issued a public denial asserting that it was done by a 'false, flattering, and lying monk'. As a result Cranmer was committed to the Tower of London and kept in prison until his execution in Oxford in 1556.

Cranmer, being archbishop, was promptly suspended from his functions and though Queen Mary wanted Cardinal Reginald Pole as primate, this had to wait for three years after her accession until

Cranmer's death by fire. As papal legate Pole absolved Parliament and later addressed the Convocations, but he was too busy to be enthroned in Canterbury in person so the ceremony took place by proxy. One of the canons residentiary represented the absent cardinal archbishop, a bad precedent which was only too often followed in years to come. An enthronement on the grand scale of Warham or even Cranmer became obsolete until modern times when it has once again been held to mark the real beginning of the reign of the Primate of All England. Pole attached far more importance to the reception of the pallium sent over from Rome. He received it at a magnificent ceremony on Lady Day in the church of St Mary le Bow in London. The following month he retired to Canterbury for diplomatic reasons. War had broken out between the papacy and Spain, and, as a result of his association with Philip and Mary, Pole was in disgrace in Rome. Only a year and twenty months after receiving the pallium he died in Lambeth Palace within a few hours of Mary Tudor herself.

His funeral ceremonies were carried out in the traditional Catholic manner, the body lying in state for forty days in Lambeth Palace while requiem Masses were said. It was then carried down to Canterbury to be received by a great concourse of the local citizens and clergy, and laid to rest in a brick tomb in the Corona. The tomb was plastered over and inscribed with the words *Depositum Cardinalis Poli*, and the wall above was painted with the Cardinal's coat of arms, the name of God in Hebrew, and the scene of the Resurrection. By the end of the nineteenth century the tomb was much dilapidated, and the inscription and mural paintings obliterated. In 1897 Cardinal Vaughan, the Roman Catholic Archbishop of Westminster, was allowed by the dean and chapter to give a large heraldic board, painted with the Cardinal's hat and arms, to hang on the wall. The tomb has recently been replastered and the words *Depositum Cardinalis Poli* reincised in gilt lettering on the front.

Cardinal Pole was the last archbishop of Canterbury to be at once a cardinal and papal legate in communion with the see of Rome, and to wear the pallium. He is remembered with affection at the King's School, where a portrait of him in stained glass can be seen in the little chapel by the Green Court Gate. In his will he bequeathed to the dean and chapter the almonry buildings around the present Mint Yard, which had been given to him by Mary Tudor, for the sake of instruction in sound learning to be held for

500 years on a nominal rent. In 1573 the scholars moved in and the Mint Yard and the adjoining buildings have been the heart and centre of the school ever since.

By a strange twist of fortune Reginald Pole was not the last cardinal to be buried near the ancient site of the shrine of St Thomas. This honour was reserved for the Cardinal de Chastillon, Odet de Coligny, Archbishop of Toulouse and Count-Bishop of Beauvais. It would be difficult to imagine a greater contrast between this French nobleman, who owed his rise in the Church to the fact that his mother was of the great and powerful house of Montmorency, and the English cardinal. Pole lived and died a devoted supporter of the papacy and the Roman Church. Coligny and his brothers went over to the Huguenot cause and were involved in the setbacks and disasters that befell that party. He lost his ecclesiastical preferments in France but seems to have retained his cardinal's hat—in a painting of him and his two brothers at Knole Park he is shown wearing a biretta with the black dress of a Huguenot gentleman. In due course he married, and in an attempt to persuade Queen Elizabeth to support the Huguenots he passed through Canterbury on his way to London in 1565.

His last visit was in 1571 when he stayed in Meister Omers, the huge monastic guesthouse which had been divided to form houses for some of the canons and their families. Here he fell ill and died, probably of tertian fever, though it was later rumoured that he had been poisoned by his valet who was in the pay of the Catholic party in France. The chapter, now presided over by Dean Godwin, clearly thought that interment of the body was merely on a temporary basis until the family were able to take it back to France. So the coffin was placed on a vacant spot in the Trinity Chapel near the tomb of Archbishop Courtenay. It was covered with a rough case of bricks and a record was not even made in the cathedral burial register, which had just been started. And there in its brick covering the coffin remains to this day, though in 1952 the Friends of the Cathedral had it tidied up and a heraldic cartouche was erected above the tomb. Given by John Dickens, and made by the sculptor Cecil Thomas, it is carved in Caen stone and adorned with the Coligny coat of arms surmounted by the red hat of the cardinal. Even with this decoration it remains one of the strangest memorials in the cathedral.

9

Elizabethan Canterbury and the Laudian Revival

The death of Queen Mary Tudor and Cardinal Pole not only spelt an end to the traditional allegiance to Rome, but also brought about a loosening of the ties that had bound the archbishops of Canterbury to their cathedral church for so long. No archbishop was to be buried in the cathedral again until 1897, and the time was coming when the primates were to cease even to have a house of their own in Canterbury. Fire had destroyed the archiepiscopal palace in 1544, and it was not rebuilt until 1565 when Archbishop Parker was firmly in possession of the see, and the settlement of the Church of England was beginning to be accepted.

Parker was one of the best archbishops of the Reformation era, though all that remains to commemorate him in the cathedral is a small coat of arms over the door leading into the north-east transept. He abandoned the traditional coat of arms of the see of Canterbury in favour of that of the cathedral church, formerly used by the monastic chapter, and by the dean and chapter to this day. This may have been from dislike of the presence of the pallium with its implications of dependence on Rome. His successors, however, reverted to the traditional coat of arms which has become one of the most familiar of all heraldic devices in modern church decoration.

With the new order, changes had to be made amongst the cathedral clergy. As usual Dean Wotton remained in office, but five of the canons residentiary were replaced. Several of the six preachers had fled the country under Mary Tudor and lost their stalls because they were married or held Protestant views. These now returned to take up office again, the most famous being Thomas Becon, one of Cranmer's chaplains, who was promoted and became a prebendary. Richard Turner, another protégé of Cranmer, was restored

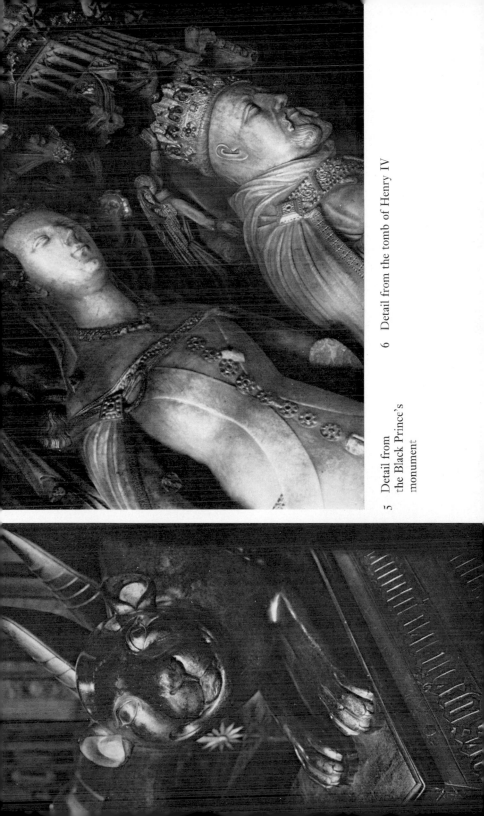

5 Detail from the Black Prince's monument

6 Detail from the tomb of Henry IV

7 Vault
of the
Water-Tower

8 The enthronement of the
hundred-and-first Archbishop of
Canterbury, 31 January, 1975

by Archbishop Parker and given a commission to visit the dioceses of Canterbury and Rochester to reform abuses.

So much of the property of the cathedral chapter, particularly vestments and plate, had been sold or stolen, that Parker had to borrow money from the Queen to take possession of his see and rebuild his derelict palace. Even some of what remained had to be sold in 1567, when Dean Godwyn succeeded Dr Wotton, to pay the stipends of the twelve minor canons. Royal occasions continued to enliven both city and cathedral as in medieval times, since part of the old Abbey of St Augustine had become a royal palace on the dissolution of the monastery, and was to remain so until after the restoration of Charles II. Queen Elizabeth stayed there and was entertained for a fortnight in 1573. A great service in the cathedral was followed four days later by a sumptuous banquet in the newly restored palace, to mark the Queen's fortieth birthday. The ancient marble chair in which she sat on this occasion was almost certainly the famous primatial throne known as St Augustine's Chair. This must have been brought out of the cathedral for the only time in history, perhaps at the Queen's command, to emphasize in Canterbury her claim as Supreme Head of the Church.

Two years later Parker died, and was succeeded by Edmund Grindal. It must have been during his primacy that the west crypt, which had stood empty and unused since the dissolution, became the spiritual headquarters of the Huguenot community. These industrious Protestants had been gathering in Canterbury from France and the Walloon districts of Belgium as refugees from the religious wars. They soon became a valuable part of the commercial population of the city, worshipping first in St Alphege Church near the palace and settling down in and around the middle of the city within the walls. It may well have been that the parish churches were too small, or unwilling to accommodate this large company of strangers who were accustomed to worship in their own French tongue and in their own Calvinist tradition. At any rate, in the last quarter of the sixteenth century, the French church in the crypt came into being, and has had an unbroken history from that day to this.

The last archbishop of Elizabeth's reign was John Whitgift. He left little mark on the cathedral, but is remembered in Canterbury as the primate who secured an Act of Parliament in 1584 establishing the old Pilgrims' Hospital of Eastbridge as an almshouse for five brothers and five sisters, with a school for boys attached in the hospital chapel. Like Archbishop Parker he plundered the cathedral library of some of its fine manuscripts to enrich the Cambridge college in which they were both interested. The Puritan George Abbot, archbishop during most of the reign of James I and the first eight years of Charles I, did his best to redress the balance by giving forty-six of his own books to the library. His coat of arms, and that of his son-in-law, William Kingsley, Archdeacon of Canterbury, can be seen in the window of the passage which links the cathedral library to the north-east transept.

Dean Godwyn had died in 1584 and his successor Dean Rogers, who was also Bishop of Dover, set a new fashion which was followed by the deans for the next century or so. He had himself buried in a handsome tomb adorned with coats of arms in the Lady Chapel off the Place of the Martyrdom, which became known as the Deans' Chapel in consequence. Here in due course appeared the tombs of Dean Nevil, moved to the south ambulatory some fifty years ago, Dean Fotherby, encrusted with skulls and bones, and Dean Boys, showing him as he died at his desk in his library in cassock, ruff, and gown, as well as the portrait on copper of Dean Bargrave and the large baroque monument of Dean Turner, a faithful supporter of the exiled Stuarts.

Following the Reformation some noteworthy memorials of scholarly canons and eminent laymen were erected in the nave. At the west end of the north aisle is the charming memorial tablet to Hadrian de Saravia, and at the east end to Richard Colfe. Both were prebendaries and men of great learning who were appointed in the latter years of Elizabeth's reign despite their foreign birth and Huguenot origin. Saravia was a Fleming, though his father was Spanish, and he was Pastor of Leyden before settling in England in 1587 where he became a champion of episcopacy. This secured him royal favour and a prebendal stall at Canterbury, Worcester, and Westminster. James I appointed him one of the translators of the Old Testament. Richard Colfe, who was vice-dean when he died, came over from Calais at the time of its capture by the French in 1558. His brother Isaac was Master of Eastbridge Hospital, and his son Abraham founded a celebrated almshouse in Lewisham. On the pavement of the south-west transept many gravestones recall other such men, no less than twelve prebendaries over this period being of French, Flemish, or Swiss origin.

Near Dr Colfe's monument is the handsome tomb of Sir John

Boys (who died in 1612). He lies full length in legal robes as befits a Recorder of Canterbury and Judge of the Claims Court of the Cinque Ports. Steward to five successive archbishops, he seems to have been a man of great piety and philanthropy, founding at the end of his life the little almshouse of Jesus Hospital in Canterbury. Next to his tomb is a hanging 'three-decker' monument, commemorating various members of the Hales family. At the top is Sir James Hales, shown being buried at sea from an Elizabethan ship of the line. He was treasurer of the naval expedition sent against Cadiz as a reprisal in the year after the Armada, and he died at sea in 1589. His wife Alice is shown kneeling in the middle of the monument and at the foot kneels Chenies his son, in a smart cutaway doublet and hose (died 1596).

On the other side of the cathedral in St Michael's Chapel, surrounding the memorials to Lady Holland and her husbands, is a fine group of monuments erected to the memory of many who died fighting in the various wars of religion which plagued Europe for nearly a century after the Reformation. Colonel Prude, whose kneeling figure can be seen just inside the chapel gate, died at the siege of Maestricht in 1632. Next to him is Sir Thomas Thornhurst, whose monument is one of the largest in the cathedral. He was killed at the siege of the island of Rhé off La Rochelle in 1627. (Commemorating a victorious warrior rather than a fallen hero is the handsome bust of Admiral Sir George Rooke, the conqueror of Gibraltar in 1704.)

One of the most important monuments in the cathedral nave is the fine portrait bust of Orlando Gibbons, the composer, who died at the early age of forty-one from apoplexy in Canterbury where he had come to superintend the musical arrangements for the wedding of Charles I to Henrietta Maria in 1625. His widow had the bust made by the celebrated sculptor Nicholas Stone at a cost of £38. It stands in a niche with a coat of arms above and an inscription below. Perhaps the most conspicuous of all the early seventeenth-century memorials is that of Alexander Chapman, canon of Canterbury and archdeacon of Stowe in the diocese of Lincoln. He was probably given these preferments because he was chaplain to Elizabeth, daughter of James I, and famous as the Winter Queen of Bohemia and mother of Prince Rupert. When he died in 1629 he was given the singular honour of a handsome memorial tablet and full-face portrait bust in the Martyrdom transept, looking down on the spot where St Thomas died and where the Altar of the Sword's Point had stood for so many centuries. Innumerable pictures and photographs have reproduced the likeness of this spare and ascetic divine looking bleakly over his ruff at the tourists below. But shortly before the Becket commemorations of 1970 the monument was taken down and later re-erected at the west end of the north ambulatory. Even here the venerable archdeacon is confronted by a celebrated and very large picture of the murder of Becket, on the opposite wall, painted by John Cross in the mid-nineteenth century.

10

Puritan Iconoclasm and the Rule of the Preachers

The reign of Charles I was dominated ecclesiastically by William Laud who was virtually primate for some years before his actual appointment. (His predecessor, George Abbot, had been suspended for accidentally shooting a keeper while out hunting.) Once enthroned, Laud concentrated on reforming the cathedral, as he intended it to be a place where all the world might see the dignity of Anglican worship. A new altar table with 'throw-over' frontal was provided as well as silver candlesticks, a lavabo bowl of silver, a Bible and Prayer Book in silver-gilt covers, and a small organ painted with the arms of Dean Bargrave which can still be seen in the cathedral library. A magnificent font was also erected, a gift from one of the prebendaries, Dr John Warner, to mark his appointment to the see of Rochester in 1639. Still one of the most conspicuous ornaments of the nave, it stands on a plinth of marble with a fine wooden cover adorned with figures of apostles and evangelists, its iron crane surmounted by the arms of Charles I.

Meanwhile, the early years of the seventeenth century saw Puritanism growing in strength and influence inside the Church of England as well as outside. No doubt the presence of many religious refugees in East Kent and Canterbury itself may have accounted for the vigorous and intemperate nature of much of this extreme Protestantism in the cathedral city. But it is impossible to acquit Archbishop Laud for much of the furious opposition to his policies. In a bigoted age he must rank among the most narrow-minded and intransigent of prelates. However much one may applaud his attempts to restore something of the beauty of worship not only in his own cathedral but to the whole Church, his way of going about it was bound to cause conflict.

The dean for most of this period was Isaac Bargrave, a prebendary of the cathedral until his preferment in 1625. The six preachers were by this time non-resident country clergy drawing a stipend and letting their houses in the precincts, riding into Canterbury to perform their preaching duties from time to time. But it would appear from the answers to questions asked by Laud in his visitation of the cathedral in 1634 that services were reasonably well ordered. In addition to the small organ, four players of brass instruments, cornetists and sackbut players, now had a place on the foundation. But the zealous archbishop was concerned to hear of the leasing of houses in the precincts to lay people, and of the disturbance caused by the holding of fairs in the precincts four times a year.

His relationship with his cathedral church is difficult to discover. Like other seventeenth-century primates he did not come to Canterbury to be enthroned, but he took a great interest in the cathedral and was in sympathy with the way its clergy were discharging their functions. He laid it down that the archbishop as visitor was

to provide diligently that the praises of God be celebrated constantly morning and evening in the Cathedral; that the most beautiful fabric as the dignity of the place demands may be preserved not from ruin only but also from defect as well without as within (to the postponement of all other matters whatsoever) and that from time to time as often as it may be necessary it may be repaired at the cost of the Church; and finally that all the members of the aforesaid Church should perform their proper office in brotherly charity, soberly and religiously.

Elsewhere, however, his vigorous and tactless attempts at reformation and his indirect interference in the religious life of Scotland raised up a vast amount of enmity against him. This opposition, together with the growing spirit of rebellion against the autocratic nature of Charles's own rule, brought about the outbreak of the Civil War and the ruin of all his work. It was typical of his propensity to meddle with matters that might well have been left alone in difficult times that he should have turned his attention to the devout Protestants of the French Church in the west crypt and endeavoured, unsuccessfully, to make them conform to Anglican ways.

In Scotland he attempted to force upon a Presbyterian nation both bishops and liturgy which were generally detested as 'rags of

Popery'. One of his protégés, James Wedderburn, Bishop of Dunblane, was among the principal architects of the new canons and Prayer Book which were intended to bring Scottish religion into line with the Church of England. But the celebrated riot which greeted the first appearance of the new liturgy in the Cathedral of St Giles in Edinburgh in 1637 set all Scotland aflame, and at the Glasgow Assembly the following year Wedderburn and all his fellow bishops were deprived and episcopacy was abolished. He fled south, settled in Canterbury, and when he died in 1639 was laid to rest under a memorial stone in the Deans' Chapel.

A few weeks after Wedderburn's death a violent storm brought down one of the newly erected weather vanes from the pinnacles on top of Bell Harry Tower. A superstitious age saw in this an omen of disaster, and on his last visit to Canterbury in 1642 King Charles climbed the tower to inspect the damage. This was very considerable, for the heavy stone pinnacle with the painted vane attached had fallen right through the cloister roof before the Martyrdom door and broken down the vault where the arms of the primacy had been. In due course the vault was repaired, and it can easily be seen where disaster struck the roof as the arms of Dean Bargrave appear among all the medieval carving and coats of arms of fifteenth-century primates.

From then on, one disaster followed hard on the heels of another. An attempt to have the Sunday sermon, beloved by the Puritans, transferred from the chapter house, where it had been preached for a number of years, back to the cathedral choir caused a near riot. Divine service was interrupted one Sunday morning by a demonstration on the part of the aggrieved congregation, some of whom sang psalms continuously during the service. The chapter wisely bowed to the rising storm and the sermon was again preached in the chapter house. It had been fitted up since the departure of the monks as a comfortable auditorium known as the sermon house, and it continued to be used for this purpose long after the restoration of Charles II.

In the struggle which was clearly impending, the cathedral authorities took sides with king and archbishop. In an area so dominated by Puritanism as East Kent it was inevitable that the cathedral itself would suffer. One can only wonder at the folly of the chapter at this stage in turning the All Saints Chapel into an armoury, and laying up there stores of armour, gunpowder, and ammunition. Puritan opposition was directed against Dean Bargrave as representative of the cathedral and when he went before Parliament to protest against a Bill for the abolition of deans and chapters, he was fined £1,000 and spent some time in the Fleet Prison.

In August 1642 the first physical onslaught on the cathedral took place. A Parliamentary officer, Colonel Sandys, arrived with a troop of horse. After assaulting the unfortunate womenfolk in the deanery, he unleashed his soldiers on the cathedral where all the ornaments that had been provided by Laud were destroyed or broken : organ, font, altar, the ancient brass lectern which had survived from monastic times, the arras hangings, and even the cassocks, surplices, and music books of the lay clerks. The soldiers finished up by firing a fusillade of shots at the great figure of Christ in the niche over Christ Church Gate before they went off to Dover.

At the end of that year King Charles and Queen Henrietta visited Canterbury and were shown the damaged font, and heard a sermon in the choir where the communion table had been set up again in its old position and other damage repaired. (The dean and chapter sold some of the altar plate and furnishings to pay the cost of the repairs.) The royal visit must have been the last occasion of importance before the Civil War and the Commonwealth. Dean Bargrave died in 1643 and later that year Parliament passed a Bill for the abolition of all capitular bodies. The next dean, Dr George Aglionby, was never installed and died within this year which saw the fall of Laud and the systematic destruction of the cathedral ornaments and windows.

The saddest and bleakest period in the history of the cathedral now began. There was no archbishop, and no dean, prebendaries or other properly ordained officers to guard and maintain the fabric or the liturgical life which had endured for over a thousand years in one form or another. However, the clerical vacuum was soon filled by, of all people, the six preachers. The Parliamentary commissioners responsible for the administration of the cathedral and its estates suddenly elevated the preachers from a very subordinate position to complete control of the daily life of the cathedral. This now consisted of sermons, biblical teaching, and extemporary prayers in place of the Book of Common Prayer.

Foremost among the six preachers who took over was Richard Culmer, known as Blue Dick because his opposition to the established order took the form of wearing a blue cassock instead of a black one. Like some of the other preachers of Puritan sympathies he was educated at the King's School, ordained into the Church of England, and then became incumbent of a parish near Canterbury. He was suspended for his opposition to Laud and held no further post until that prelate's fall. In an extraordinary pamphlet which he published, called *Cathedral News from Canterbury*, he describes in the third person how he launched an assault on the cathedral ornaments and stained glass as one of the cathedral commissioners appointed to purify the building. His prime targets were the statues over the choir door and on the north door of the choir and, above all, the great window of the Martyrdom transept. Given by Edward IV, it was one of the glories of the cathedral, with its enormous figures of St Thomas of Canterbury and Our Lady and the Blessed Trinity. By the time Culmer, perched on a tall ladder with a pike, had finished rattling down 'Becket's glassy bones', in his own choice phrase, not much remained of Neve's splendid glass except the tracery figures (which were probably too high for him to reach), some heraldry, and the kneeling figures of the royal family.

Culmer himself had applied to Parliament in 1644 for the stall of a preacher and got it on the grounds that he was a godly divine and most fitted to preach in the cathedral. He was joined in 1648 by Thomas Ventriss who had been curate to Archdeacon Kingsley, then by John Player and Thomas Hieron, both ordained priests of Puritan sympathies. Two other preachers, Francis Taylor, who was blind, and John Durrant, may well have been nonconformist ministers. They also were given rectories in Canterbury at the expense of the sitting incumbents who were turned out for loyalty to the old régime.

While the preachers ran the services in the cathedral and chapter house, Parliamentary sequestrators managed the estates of archbishop and chapter which had been confiscated. They let the houses of the clergy in the precincts to lay people, but paid pensions to the former clergy and salaries to the other members of the foundation, as well as maintaining the fabric in tolerable repair. Among those who deserve to be well remembered were Captain Thomas Monins who was the treasurer general, and John Cogan who headed a local committee for the administration of church lands and founded a hospital for the widows of six poor clergy in the city.

A fascinating picture of the cathedral at this time was to be seen in a painting exhibited at the Tate Gallery in the winter of 1972–3.

61

Signed by Thomas Johnson and dated 1657, it shows Puritans at work in the cathedral choir destroying stained glass and ornaments. The choir is shown devoid of all furniture. Throne, altar, lectern, all have vanished, but the painting gives a vivid impression of the vast and splendid building with its ascending flights of steps, iron grilles, tombs, and monuments, and a good deal of mural painting on vault and walls. Apart from the archbishop's palace which fell into ruin and remained out of use for the next two and a half centuries, and the former chapel of the prior which was pulled down, surprisingly little damage was done to the buildings of the precincts. The nave seems to have been treated like a barracks, with 3,000 arms and 300 horses kept there, and the postern and other gates were mured up for the defence of the city. Parliament abolished Christmas Day and all other festivals, and on Christmas Day 1647 Edward Aldey, royalist vicar of St Andrew's, caused a riot in the city by preaching a sermon in his church. At the same time the mayor tried to make all the people open their shops, and it eventually needed a great company of trained men quartered in the city to bring the citizens of Canterbury to heel.

11

Church and Crown Restored in Canterbury

When the monarchy was restored in 1660 the obvious choice as archbishop was William Juxon, who had attended Charles I as chaplain at his execution. Thomas Turner, appointed dean in 1643 but never allowed to take up office, was installed as well as twelve prebendaries. Only three had survived from former days, the other nine being new appointments. One was Peter Gunning, later Bishop of Chichester and then of Ely, who is reputed to have written the lovely prayer 'for all sorts and conditions of men' in the 1662 Prayer Book. Another was Edward Aldey, whose Christmas sermon had caused a furore.

Charles II made his triumphant entry into Canterbury in May 1660. When he went to service in the choir, the Prayer Book was heard again in public worship for the first time for at least seventeen years. He stayed in the palace, formerly the Abbey of St Augustine, which was cleaned up and repaired for the event, and the citizens presented him with a golden cup. The preachers were removed from their stalls and their houses, and replaced by clergy who had been loyal to the Crown.

When the new chapter assembled in the autumn, they had to cope with disordered finances and a building in disrepair, devoid of ornaments or the essential furniture for public worship. One of the most battered of the ancillary buildings was the Christ Church Gate which had had its doors torn off; and the great statue of Christ in the niche over the gate had been lassooed and pulled down by the soldiers. (The niche has remained empty to this day.) All the statues in the cathedral had vanished except for the Six Kings on the stone screen at the entrance to the choir.

New doors were made for Christ Church Gate, adorned with the arms of the new archbishop and dean. A handsome brass lectern of traditional eagle type, costing £8, was made by William Borroghes. But the first charge on the revenues was the purchase of plate to replace all that had gone. Quite a lot of this survives in use today including an alms dish of 1663, two pricket candlesticks for the High Altar of the same date, a chalice and paten, and a flagon of 1665.[1] The oldest pieces of silver appear to be two vergers' maces of 1660 with the arms of the see on one side and of the dean and chapter on the other. These, together with a Bible in silver-gilt covers, were given by Dean Turner on the occasion of his installation as a thank-offering for deliverance from a great danger. They suggest that cathedral services with traditional ceremonial were restored at once, and the accounts show that the full choral foundation was functioning again by the end of 1660. The purchase of chafing dishes and frankincense points to the use of incense in the post-Reformation cathedral, perhaps for sanitary rather than ceremonial purposes.

In the years following their return, the chapter spent the great sum of £8,000 on the repair of the cathedral and its refurnishing, as well as £1,000 on putting in order the deanery and houses of residentiary canons and other Church officers, while the stipends of the lay clerks were increased. In place of the old Prior's Chapel a handsome library in mellow brick was built by order of Arch-bishop Juxon. The great collection of books which had vanished could now be replaced, and gifts of money and books from Bishop Warner, Archbishop Sancroft, and William Somner were the basis of the restored library. (It was Somner, author of the great work, *The Antiquities of Canterbury*, dedicated to Archbishop Laud on its publication in 1640, who is said to have gathered up the broken pieces of the font after the Puritans had smashed it, and concealed them until the Restoration, when he returned them to the cathedral.)

One of the most interesting additions to the cathedral was a picture of King Charles the Martyr which hung over the western door of the choir. Placed now on the north side of the choir ambula-tory, it shows him forsaking an earthly crown for a heavenly one. The work of reparation must have been both speedy and thorough, for in January 1665 John Evelyn could write in his diary about a visit to Canterbury, 'I arrived and went to the cathedral exceedingly well repaired since His Majesty's return.' This must have been a relief since he had recorded of a visit in October 1641, 'I visited the

---

[1] These were made by a Mr Dale in London and sent down by water to Faversham.

cathedral then in great splendour those famous windows being intire, since demolished by the phanatiqs.'

Among the new six preachers was a nephew of old Dean Bargrave, Dr John Bargrave, a man of great ability who was soon promoted to a prebendal stall. He was responsible for the erecting of a fine wall monument to his uncle, with a picture of the dean painted on copper and attributed to Cornelius Jansen. This was placed on the north wall of the Deans' Chapel in 1679 and has recently been moved to a blank wall on the opposite side of the chapel. There it faces an equally handsome mural monument to Dean Turner, placed on the east wall at his death in 1672 with such insensitivity, however, that a lovely fifteenth-century cornice showing angels holding lettered scrolls was virtually wiped out. The moving of the Turner monument to the north wall has now enabled this frieze to be seen again after 300 years. It has in the middle a beautiful gilded and painted angel bearing a scroll with the words *Gloria Tua* upon it.

Dr Bargrave, the dean's nephew, was one of the most interesting and attractive of the clergy who came on to the foundation at the Restoration. From the King's School he went on to Cambridge where he became a Fellow of Peterhouse until he was removed under the Puritan régime. He wisely exiled himself to Italy to study at the University of Padua, and there still exists in his own hand in the cathedral library a wonderful account of Rome and the cardinals, as well as books he bequeathed to it. After he became a prebendary, he travelled to Algiers on a mission of rescue, ransoming English prisoners who were sold as slaves. 'I bought them slave by slave as one bought horses in Smithfield ... (167 in all) but it was a thousand to one that I and my fellow commissioner had been made slaves' he wrote on his return, having spent £340 on this errand of mercy. After his burial under a slab on the Martyrdom floor, now almost defaced, one of the fetters from the limbs of a ransomed slave was placed over his tomb.

In 1675 the dean, then the celebrated preacher Dr Tillotson, later to be archbishop, decided with the chapter to wainscot the choir against the parclose screens erected some three and a half centuries before by Prior Eastry. Roger Davis, master joiner of London, was employed to do the work which, from contemporary pictures, was very handsomely done. In 1682 the chapter commissioned him, at a cost of £320, to place at the west end of the choir, against the stone screen, the set of twelve return stalls. (The success of this work may have led to Roger Davis being chosen as one of the crafts-men to make the stalls, screens, and galleries for St Paul's Cathedral.) Victorian taste swept away the wainscoting and Sir Gilbert Scott prepared plans for replacing the return stalls with others of a dull Gothic design like those to be seen in several English cathedrals which fell into his hands. But his plans were not accepted and the splendid return stalls still remain, adorned with the arms of Charles II, Archbishop Sheldon (who had succeeded Juxon in 1663), and the dean and chapter.

Other gifts which still remain in use are the fine candelabra, now electrified, hanging from the vaults of choir and transepts. One was given in 1692 by Sir Anthony Aucher, another in 1726 by Archdeacon Tenison, and a third in 1747 by Prebendary Shuck-ford.

By the time the stalls were finished Charles II was dead and James II's troubled reign had begun, while Sancroft had succeeded Sheldon as archbishop. He is remembered at Canterbury as the donor of a charming silver mace which is borne before the arch-deacons on Ascension Day, when by statute they preach at the morning service, and when they hold their visitations in the cathedral. He was a rather sad figure for, having headed the proces-sion of the Seven Bishops to the Tower and won vast popularity thereby, he felt unable to take the oath of allegiance to William and Mary and so he was deprived of his great office to become one of the most eminent of the non-jurors.

With the accession of William and Mary, we enter upon a period in the religious history of England which was to last for a century and a half, when the life of the Church sank lower and lower. Dull mediocrities filled the great offices, notably the Chair of St Augustine, as well as the deaneries and prebendal stalls of every cathedral in the land. Canterbury was no exception to the general rule, but events of importance did happen and people who mattered did come to the cathedral. If only in a negative way, the era of Enlightenment has left its mark on the fabric and the precincts.

PART III

---

*The Long Sleep and the
Great Awakening*

12

From Queen Anne to Queen Victoria

In the early years of the eighteenth century, the royal arms were set up in many of the city churches of Canterbury as a mark of loyalty to the good Anglican Queen Anne, a grand-daughter of the sainted royal martyr, Charles I. In the cathedral choir the old monastic stalls which had survived the Commonwealth were replaced by solid pews and dignified wainscoting. Outside, the spire on the Norman north-west tower, much damaged by the great storm of 1703, was taken down, though the tower itself was to remain until the reign of William IV. In the south-west tower in 1726 was placed a ring of eight bells cast by Samuel Knight of Holborn. Considering how slender were the ties that bound Canterbury to its non-resident archbishops at this time, it is pleasant to record the munificent gift of a handsome throne for the choir in 1704, often said to have been carved by Grinling Gibbons himself. This was a gift from Archbishop Tenison who revived the ancient ceremony of enthronement in 1695, first stating 'that he was satisfied there was nothing dependent on it'. His throne was a carved wooden canopy on Corinthian columns with a red plush chair below, and it remained in the choir in the traditional position on the south side until 1844 when the present throne replaced it. Since no sign of the ancient throne can be seen in Thomas Johnson's picture of the choir dated 1657, it must be presumed that the Puritans demolished it and that the Tenison throne was a somewhat belated replacement over forty years after the Restoration of the Stuarts. This throne can now be seen just inside the south-west door of the nave.

Not all benefactions were as worth while as Tenison's throne. In 1729 Dr Grandorge, one of the prebendaries, left £500 which was used for making a new altarpiece designed by James Burrough, a Cambridge don. When this was set in place in 1733 it turned out to be of a heavy classical design, and the chapter thereupon brought the choir into line with the new altarpiece. Wainscoting was put round the whole presbytery area and the tombs of the archbishops on each side vanished from sight behind the panelling. (This was, fortunately, removed by their successors in 1825.) A well-to-do widow, Mrs Nixon, and her nephew Herbert Randolph, one of the six preachers, produced enough money between them to pay for the laying of a new black and white marble pavement round the altar. And Captain Humphrey Pudnor, a retired naval officer, gave a large sum of money to the chapter in an endeavour to tidy up the exterior of the Corona, unfinished at the dissolution in 1540.

Archbishop Wake is one of the most interesting of the eighteenth-century primates. A stickler for doing things properly, he revived the customs attached to the election and enthronement of an arch-bishop which had been largely allowed to disappear. On the death of Tenison in December 1715, the dean and chapter were asked to petition the Crown for the right to elect an archbishop. The *congé d'élire* was received on 31 December, and they proceeded to elect Wake formally on 5 January, the confirmation of the election following on 16 January in the church of St Mary le Bow in Cheap-side. The enthronement took place on 15 June, the Archbishop robing in the consistory court which was under the old Romanesque tower at the north-west corner of the nave. The Dean, Dr Stanhope, and the Vice-Dean escorted the Archbishop to the seat which Tenison had placed under its canopy on the south-east side of the choir. There the Archdeacon, Dr Thomas Green, enthroned him after a royal mandate had been read by a notary public. After Morning Prayer had been sung and a sermon preached by one of the preben-daries, the Dean and the Vice-Dean escorted the Primate to the Marble Chair at the east end of the choir. The Archdeacon enthroned him there, taking him afterwards to the Dean's Stall. The Te Deum sung by the choir, followed by versicles, responses, and collect, ended the proceedings in the cathedral. The procession of the foundation then went to place the Archbishop in the Prior's seat in the chapter house and there to make to him the promise of canonical obedience, the Archdeacon for the fourth time performing the actual ceremony of installation. It seems to have been a solemn occasion, and it is sad to record that no primate thought it worth while following Wake's example until the enthronement of Sumner in 1848, since when every archbishop has been enthroned in the traditional manner.

Dr Wake followed his enthronement with a visitation of the dean and chapter on the very next day, preached in the cathedral, and entertained the mayor and aldermen of the city on 17 June; and on 19 June he proceeded to visit the deaneries of the diocese one by one. His visitation of the cathedral was searching and throws some light on the cathedral clergy and the life of the cathedral at that time. There were twelve articles of inquiry mostly concerned with the residence of the chapter and the finances. From the answers it appears that there were usually as many as four, five, or even six prebendaries in residence at any given time, out of the twelve members of the chapter. The precentor kept a daily record of attendance which was read out at the chapter meeting once a fortnight, fines being levied for absence quarterly. The minor canons, whose number had been reduced to six in the seventeenth century, had a good record for attendance at the daily offices. Holy Communion was at this period celebrated every Sunday and on Christmas Day. The chapter had set £200 aside for repairs and £100, together with the Communion alms, was allotted to the poor. The fabric was in good repair, and the King's School in good state as to masters and boys. The archbishop made a great point of the desirability of the Litany being sung not said, and at a later visitation in 1724 he insisted on the prebendaries residing in their houses, and laid it down as important that only learned priests (men with a university degree) should be invited to preach from the cathedral pulpit.

The last years of the eighteenth century saw few changes in the life of the cathedral. The Holy Communion was celebrated each week until 1790 when the weekly celebration became a monthly one. The daily sung services were resumed immediately after the Restoration of 1660, Mattins at 10 a.m. and Evensong at 3 p.m. in summer and 4 p.m. in winter. Early prayers were said in the chapter house which continued to be used as a sermon house. Much information about life in Canterbury at this period is provided in A Walk In and About the City of Canterbury, published by William Gostling, one of the minor canons, in 1774.

With the coming of the nineteenth century, echoes of the Napoleonic Wars began to be heard in the quiet world of the precincts. A foretaste is the stone tablet in the Martyrdom to Captain Thomas Piercy who in 1779 protected a convoy of merchant ships against a French fleet led by the American privateer Paul Jones. The memorials in the south aisle of the nave are like a roll-call of

Wellington's victories in the Peninsular War. Lt.-Col. Stuart died at Rolera, Lt.-Col. Sir William Inglis was appointed Colonel for gallantry at the battle of Albuera, and Lt.-Col. Charles Taylor died at Vimiera. The final episodes in the war with France are documented by the memorials of Captain John Purvis of the Royal Scots Regiment who fell at the siege of Bergen-op-Zoom in 1814, Lt. Erskine Fraser, killed at the siege of San Sebastian in 1813, and Robert Macpherson Cairnes, 'taken from this sublunary scene on June 18th, 1815 when he fell on the plains of Waterloo'.

A coat of arms is emblazoned with the word 'Trafalgar' over a window in the north clerestory at the west end of the nave. It looks out of place in its very medieval surroundings but the explanation is simple. At Nelson's death in 1805 all his titles, including that of Duke of Bronte, passed to his older brother, William, a bucolic clergyman who had been made a canon residentiary of Canterbury in 1803, no doubt because of the Admiral's influence. The College of Arms devised for him armorial bearings in the appalling taste of the day, commemorating among other episodes in Admiral Nelson's career his greatest naval triumph. In the time of Dean Percy it was decided to repaint the various medieval coats of arms that adorn the nave. Since some of these had lost their tincture, the blank shields were painted with the arms of the dean and prebendaries.

Hardly less bizarre than the coat of arms of Dr William Nelson is that of Canon Edward Pellew. He became a prebendary in 1822 while still young and went on to be Dean of Norwich. He was the third son of Viscount Exmouth who, after distinguished service at sea during the Napoleonic Wars, crowned his career in 1816 by sailing into the harbour at Algiers and bombarding the piratical Dey into submission. This resulted in the release of 3,000 Christian slaves, and Lord Exmouth was honoured by the Pope and the Catholic sovereigns of Europe. It resulted, also, in the most fantastic of all coats of arms, with a representation of Algiers and a British man-of-war. This coat, which Canon Pellew inherited from his father, is in the south aisle in the third bay from the west wall.

The passion for opening tombs which distinguished nineteenth-century chapters seems to have begun in Canterbury as early as 1832. The tomb of Henry IV and his queen, Joan of Navarre, was opened with the permission of Dean Bagot, who was Bishop of Oxford. It was believed that the body of the king had been thrown overboard on the way to Canterbury by sea to Faversham as a gale had attacked the ship and terrified the sailors. The fear that the tomb was an empty sepulchre was quickly disproved when the king's coffin, lapped in lead, was found under the pavement (the tomb had been reopened in 1437 so that the coffin of Queen Joan could be laid on top). A piece of lead was cut out in order to afford sight of the king's bearded head. After this identification the tomb was sealed up again and subsequently repaired at the government's expense.

In 1792, while France was obsessed with revolutionary fervour, Dean Buller and his chapter decided to rearrange the early Gothic glass from the choir clerestory in the great window of the south-west transept. They entrusted the work to William Burgys, the vesturer, who removed twenty-four of the genealogical figures and placed them in their new position, filling in the spaces with a miscellany of early Gothic fragments and later coats of arms. In the time of Dean Powys a similar transference of genealogical figures, some thirteen in all, was made to the west window of the nave. The spaces were again filled with small figures of saints and coats of arms of the fifteenth century.

But outside the comfortable world of the precincts and the prosperous merchants' houses of the old city, there was widespread poverty and unrest in the surrounding country among the peasants. This burst out in a rebellion headed by a mad demagogue who called himself Sir William Courtenay, Knight of Malta. The tragic end to this episode which took place a few miles out of Canterbury is commemorated by a tablet in the north aisle of the nave to Lt. Henry Boswell Bennett of the Forty-fifth Regiment. He had been sent with some soldiers to arrest the 'knight' and his followers, but was shot dead on 13 May 1838 and accorded the honours of a cathedral funeral.

This was during the primacy of William Howley, the last of the prince archbishops. He wore a wig and on state occasions was accustomed to drive in a carriage drawn by six black horses. As the prelate, who had the singular honour of baptizing, confirming, crowning, and marrying Queen Victoria, as well as announcing to her the news of the death of her uncle, William IV, and her accession to the throne, he may be regarded as a personal link between two eras. At his death in 1848 the Victorian age was well under way, the Gothic Revival in full swing, and the Oxford Movement beginning to make its mark on the Church of England.

13

Reform and Revival in the
Victorian Age

Archbishop Howley was seldom seen in Canterbury after the celebrated occasion when he was mobbed in the streets for his opposition
to the Reform Bill of 1832. Yet in many ways the two decades of
his primacy were among the most important in the modern history
of the cathedral. In 1831 the dean and chapter decided to pull down
the old Romanesque north-west tower which was all that remained
of Lanfranc's nave and façade. They procured an Act of Parliament
for this purpose, and their surveyor George Austin built an exact
copy of the adjacent south-west tower at a cost of over £24,000.
This brought Canterbury into line with other English cathedrals
like York and Wells with symmetrical western towers balancing a
grand central tower, and gave to it the famous exterior so often
painted and photographed ever since.

Earlier in the century, at the behest of Alderman Simmonds, who
created the Dane John Gardens of the city, the twin turrets of the
Christ Church Gate were demolished on the pretext that they were
structurally insecure. The Gate continued to moulder away until
some forty years ago, when the stonework, turrets, and heraldic
colouring of this splendid Tudor building were renewed in a large-
scale modern restoration. Austin also designed the great mock Gothic
throne in the choir, a gift from Howley in 1844, which replaced the
Tenison throne of 1704.

In 1848, a monument to Howley himself, showing him in the
1837 Coronation cope, was placed in the space between the tombs
of Chichele and Bourchier in the presbytery, where once the great
relics cupboard of the monks had stood. The portion of Prior Eastry's
screen which stood there was moved in due course to the entrance
of St Andrew's Chapel where it still stands. Richard Westmacott the

younger executed this memorial to Howley, who was to be the first of a line of notable Victorian primates buried in Addington churchyard near their country palace and commemorated by cenotaphs in their cathedral church. In recent years a bust of Howley by Sir Francis Chantrey was acquired by the Friends of the Cathedral and can now be seen in the cathedral library. A picture of Howley crowning Queen Victoria appears in the west window of the chapter house, and his name is also commemorated in the great collection of books known as the Howley-Harrison Library, housed in the fine red brick building on the site of the old Prior's Chapel.

Despite his disapproval, the age of Howley saw the beginning of sweeping ecclesiastical reforms which changed the whole face of the Church of England. Dean Carpenter in his book *Cantuar* claims that these would have been even more sweeping if it had not been for Howley's membership of the Ecclesiastical Commission set up by Peel's government in 1836, his wise handling of the situation, and his support for the Commission's recommendations. As a result of the work of this Commission and its survey of the country's cathedrals, the twelve prebendal stalls at Canterbury were reduced to six, the reductions taking effect as the holders of the stalls died. The six canons who remained as the administrators of the foundation were henceforth known as the residentiaries, and the title of prebendary was dropped.

This attenuated band was gradually augmented by the creation of the office of honorary canon, the numbers gradually rising over the next century to the present figure of twenty-seven. The rights and privileges of the six preachers were confirmed to them, and the number of minor canons dropped to four. The title of vice-dean which had been held since the Reformation by one of the senior canons permanently, was now held in rotation by whichever canon was in residence. As a result of all this reform the cathedral revenues were reduced drastically by the Commission, and the money was used to augment the stipends of other clergy. This was to have most unfortunate results later in the century when the value of money diminished, while the revival of Church life caused much greater demands to be made on Canterbury and other cathedrals.

As the clergy no longer needed them some of the old prebendal houses in the precincts were demolished. Amongst them were those built into the arches of the Norman infirmary in the Brick Walk which gives that part of the precincts its present appearance. The removal a few yards eastwards of the Romanesque arch which had led into the monks' cemetery in medieval times, provided a charming entrance to the canons' bowling green. (It was to become a War Memorial Garden in the next century.)

Dean Rowe Lyall was called on to preside over the enthronement of Howley's successor. Archbishop John Bird Sumner, to universal applause, announced his intention of going back to the ancient practice, revived abortively by Dr Wake, of being enthroned in person. The great ceremony took place before a vast congregation in May 1848, Sumner delivering his sermon from the new throne, in use for the first time for an enthronement.

The gradual change of atmosphere is recorded in the Acts of Chapter, a great manuscript book in the cathedral archives which begins in 1854 and ends in 1970. In the early days much time and space was taken up with managing the chapter estates, but eventually the Commissioners took over this side of cathedral life. The entries are then more concerned with installation of new canons, six preachers, a new dean, or an enthronement. The first enthronement recorded was that of Sumner's successor, Charles Longley, who gave his address from the dean's stall, all other ceremonies following the precedent set previously. Dr Longley, commemorated by a modest tablet in the nave, in 1867 summoned the first Lambeth Conference. Under his successor, Dr Tait, began the practice of having a great service in the cathedral at the opening of the Lambeth Conference every ten years.

At this service, held in the choir, the Marble Chair is usually placed before the High Altar so that the Primate of All England can welcome and address his fellow bishops from all over the Anglican Communion in a fitting manner. As the British Empire grew and expanded all through the reign of Queen Victoria, strong links were forged between the growing Church overseas and the great cathedral which many regarded as the Mother Church of them all. Many bishops were consecrated for overseas service in the cathedral, and the foundation of St Augustine's College nearby in 1848 strengthened this connection. In the south aisle of the nave a handsome tomb of medieval style commemorates the first Metropolitan of Australia, William Grant Boughton, an Old King's Scholar, who died while on a visit to England in 1853. Near him is a bust of another Old King's Scholar, Sir George Gipps, a veteran of the Peninsular War, who later became Governor of New South Wales and gave his name to the Gippsland Territory. Opposite his bust is the 'Gothic' tomb of Archbishop Sumner, and also a bust of Dr Welfitt, canon and vice-dean, who held office for forty-seven years. All these monuments were the work of another Old King's Scholar, the sculptor Henry Weekes.

Canon Welfitt was a shining example of clerical piety in a slack age, for he lived in his house in the precincts for nine months of the year, as well as regularly attending the Daily Offices. Long after reforms which began to take effect at the beginning of Victoria's reign, absenteeism was as rife in Canterbury as in Trollope's Barchester. Though theoretically allowed only three months' non-residence a year, at the annual Audit of St Catherine the residentiaries regularly drew up a rota so that each should reside for two consecutive months annually followed by six months' non-residence. One of the principal offenders was the well-known Victorian divine, Canon A. P. Stanley, later a famous Dean of Westminster. However, he placed all lovers of Canterbury in his debt by his charming book *Historical Memorials of Canterbury Cathedral*, a series of lectures on St Augustine, St Thomas Becket, and the Black Prince. This may have helped to revive interest in the cathedral and even to focus attention on its dilapidated and neglected state.

Ten years before Stanley began to give his lectures, an account in the *Ecclesiologist* for 1845 noted with disgust that

a beautiful staircase turret to the south-east transept is entirely out of repair; and generally in this part the windows are broken or their sills are vegetating with weeds; St Anselm's chapel especially requires the glazier. The northern side of the cathedral which is concealed very much by buildings is even deficient in rain-water pipes, and the walls are streaked with green. The most valuable sculptures are here unheeded, the Chapter House is in disorder, damp and littered and looked as if it were of no use in the modern economy of the cathedral.

The writer goes on to describe the cloisters used as a dumping place for ladders, tackle, and stone

in spite of the noble offers made (as we understand) in its favour by one of the canons. How unlike its former appearance when it was used for devout meditations, its windows glazed and its

77

walls painted with holy texts. The state of the crypt would not suggest to anyone that it is the resting place of some of the most illustrious Primates of the English Church.

This could have been written about any or all of the English cathedrals and many of the ancient parish churches of the land at this time. It is not surprising in view of the tradition of canonical non-residence which still survived from the early days, and the existence of such people as James Croft, Archdeacon of Canterbury, reputed at his death to have earned £160,000 from his numerous preferments. But there were good men like Dr Welfitt (who may have been the generous canon willing to restore the cloisters), and the learned Benjamin Harrison. Archdeacon of Maidstone, and author of one of the famous 'Tracts for the Times', Harrison bequeathed to the cathedral a library of 12,000 volumes, many of which he had inherited from Archbishop Howley.

When Dean Rowe Lyall died in 1856 and was buried in a grandiose tomb close to the north door of the nave, a strong successor was appointed. This was the hirsute and energetic Henry Alford, mostly remembered now for his hymns, and commemorated by an indifferent statue on the West Front. Under his leadership new statutes were issued for the government of the cathedral, and the Ecclesiastical Commissioners took over the management of the extensive estates still held by the chapter. This gave the cathedral clergy more time to devote to their spiritual work, and the results slowly began to be seen. For the first time sermons were ordered to be preached at Evensong on Sundays, the duties eventually devolving on the honorary canons and six preachers.

But even after fourteen years of Alford's energetic rule the daily services seem to have been very perfunctorily performed. A correspondent wrote to the *Church Times* in 1874 that

this cathedral equals if it does not excel any in the land in slovenliness. In many of the seats it is impossible to kneel ... and what is most striking is the disgraceful way in which the lay clerks and choristers are robed. One perhaps would hardly hope to find cassocks in use, but at least one might expect to find the surplices moderately clean and of a decent fit. Such however is very far from being the case. I was present at Evensong on the feast of St Matthew and when the procession straggled in, a more untidy

78

and illfitting set of surplices could not have been seen, many of them not even having the recommendation of cleanliness.

The seating situation was altered five years later, though whether it was improved remains a controversial point. In 1879 the eighteenth-century stalls and pews in the choir which had replaced the monastic stalls a century and a half before were in turn replaced by the present rather dull range of stalls complete with carved misericords designed by Sir Gilbert Scott. One of the illustrations to this book shows the choir with the old system of seating still in position, and many today may be disposed to question whether the Victorian chapter would not have done better to leave things as they were.

About this time the staircase known as the Dean's Stairs was erected, linking the Dark Entry with the north-east transept, and a handsome library was created out of the remains of the Norman dormitory built in Lanfranc's day. (It was to be bombed out of existence less than a century later, in 1942.) Across the Green Court the old monastic brewhouse became a school house for the cathedral choristers. This continued as a day school until the refoundation of 1936 moved it into the Table Hall in the Brick Walk, and it became largely a boarding school. Other buildings which vanished were the red-brick eighteenth-century Audit House, where the chapter used to gather for the regular audits of accounts, and the monastic Chequer House. Here only the tower was spared, to await the rebuilding of 1964 when the old ruin became part of the handsome new Wolfson Library.

In 1869 Dr A. C. Tait was enthroned as archbishop with traditional ceremony and before a huge congregation. One of his first acts was to revive the old office of Suffragan Bishop of Dover which had lapsed with the death of Dr Rogers who had also been Dean. The new Bishop was Edward Parry, son of an heroic Arctic explorer, appointed in 1869. He was also made Canon and Archdeacon of Canterbury, and after many years of devoted service to the diocese for which he was greatly beloved, he was buried in yet another mock Gothic tomb in the nave. All through the latter part of the century George Austin and his assistants, the Caldwell family, were at work filling up the windows with Victorian Gothic glass in imitation of the thirteenth-century roundels and panels destroyed by the Puritans. These windows cast 'a dim religious light' over large

79

portions of the cathedral until their destruction by enemy action in 1942.

On Alford's death in 1871 Dr Robert Payne-Smith became dean. In his time the present High Altar was erected at the top of the steps leading to the Trinity Chapel where once the Marble Chair had stood. Massive brass rails were later placed in the old position of the altar below. Dean Payne-Smith initiated the Sunday evening service with sermon which has remained a feature of the cathedral life to this day. To counter very natural complaints from the parish churches in the city a part of the collections taken at this service was ordered to be sent to them, a practice which ceased some years ago. It was fitting, therefore, that at his death in 1895 a handsome pulpit should be erected in his memory in the nave. Designed in his best Gothic manner by the great Victorian architect G. F. Bodley, it was equipped with a tester, some good carving, and figures of mitred archbishops on each side of the staircase. Its great significance lies in the fact that it was placed in the nave, for so long an empty vestibule to the choir, gradually filled up with Victorian monuments and regimental memorials. But now once more the nave began to be used for worship, as Victorian enthusiasm and energy brought the Church of England and its cathedrals to life again. For the next hundred years signs of this new life and devotion were to be seen as chapels long bare and disused were restored and brought back to use for early celebrations of Holy Communion and other devotional occasions.

Eighteen months after Dr Payne-Smith's installation, a plumber working on the roof of the Trinity Chapel upset a pot of burning charcoal which melted the lead on the roof and set fire to the rafters. The scene which ensued must have been not unlike that chronicled by Gervase almost seven centuries earlier. A contemporary account relates that

> just after the morning service at the cathedral volumes of smoke were seen issuing from the roof of the Trinity Chapel; an alarm was immediately raised: and the organist, lay clerks, and choristers at once rushed from the choir in their surplices, but they quickly returned and removed the books to the Library; meanwhile the organ blower on hearing the alarm had the presence of mind to ring Bell Harry, thus attracting the notice of the citizens.

Flames as well as dense masses of smoke which completely enveloped the central tower were now seen bursting through the east end of the roof: soon the whole city and neighbourhood was in a state of alarm and confusion.

Nearly an hour and a half elapsed before even a drop of water could be got to bear upon the burning timbers. Meanwhile the greatest alarm prevailed and the entire roof eastwards of St Andrew's and St Anselm's Chapels became the prey of devouring flames. By the time the Canterbury Volunteer Fire Brigade got to work with hoses the fire was well under way. Already the weather cock and the burning timbers of the east end of the roof had fallen in upon the groined ceiling whilst the molten lead was pouring down like streams of water and running through the joints of vaulting into the Trinity Chapel; sparks and embers were also dropping into the chapel while willing hands with all possible haste were removing everything inflammable. The armour and shield of the Black Prince were taken down, the heavy communion table was dragged away and the altar rails torn up. It was now determined to arrest the progress of the flames by cutting a vast gap in the choir roof, but it became evident that the water was gaining the upper hand and the intention was therefore abandoned. By two o'clock a ringing cheer from the soldiers and firemen on the roof rent the air and the crowd below, when they discovered that the brave men had succeeded in extinguishing the great body of the flames, heartily joined in the shout of triumph. The grand old church was saved. Only the roof of the Trinity Chapel was destroyed; the interior had been protected by the vaulted stone ceiling which was itself loaded with the charred timbers and debris.

Yet another fire menaced the cathedral a few years later, in 1876, this time at the opposite end of the cathedral in the south-west tower where the clock is to be found under the bells. Fortunately the fire which broke out while the clock was being cleaned was extinguished rapidly before it had time to spread, but with some loss of life.

An entry in the Acts of Chapter in 1878 records that the Revd F. J. O. Helmore was installed as a minor canon. He remained in office for the best part of sixty years, dying only in 1938, and for much of that time was not only precentor but also an enthusiastic campanologist. When the bells were rehung in 1897 in commemoration of the coming of Augustine 1,300 years before, and quarter chimes were added, Mr Helmore composed a chime based on the Third Gregorian Tone. This has now become famous and can be heard at Merton College, Oxford, and in other places where bells ring out the quarters and hours. (This may have been in tribute to his father Thomas who was one of the great pioneers in the revival of Gregorian music.) Strangely enough, despite its long history, it is only in modern times that the cathedral has had very eminent organists and choirmasters.[1] Dr W. H. Longhurst was organist from 1873 to 1898, and since he was a capable musician it was decided that an organ worthy of the cathedral and its increasing use for great services must be provided. So the organ of three manuals and thirty speaking stops put in by Samuel Greene in 1784 was scrapped and a fine new four-manual organ by Father Henry Willis, took its place. Apart from the four manuals and pedals, it had fifty-two speaking stops, the pipes being placed in the south triforium gallery and connected with the console immediately below by electro-pneumatic action, giving excellent service in this position for the next half-century.

Archbishop Tait died in 1882, and was buried with his predecessors at Addington. He was commemorated in the cathedral by a handsome cenotaph executed in the Italian style associated with the Cosmati family in the thirteenth century. The inscription, in the north-east transept, sums up his primacy:

A great Archbishop, just, discerning, dignified, statesmanlike: wise to know the time and resolute to redeem it. He had one mission, to make the Church of England more and more the Church of the people, drawing towards it both by word and example all who love things true and pure, beautiful and of good report.

The reclamation of the crypt began in the last part of the century. The east crypt had been used as a coal cellar ever since the chapter had granted the wily ex-monk Dr Thornden, Vice-Dean and later Bishop of Dover, the use of 'ye vault called Bishop Beckett's tomb under Our Ladye's Chappell' for wood and other firing. Now it was purged of its rubbish, the dividing walls were pulled down,

[1] With the possible exception of George Marson, a well-known madrigalist in the time of James I.

a proper floor was laid, and the noble proportions of the great double columns and Early English vaulting were revealed. The Huguenot congregation which had used the west crypt since the time of Elizabeth was persuaded to withdraw into the Black Prince's Chantry and free the whole of the lovely Norman undercroft for Anglican worship. Since their numbers had shrunk from the 2,500 recorded in Elizabeth's time to a small remnant, they were probably quite glad of the more intimate atmosphere of the chantry.

The reopening of these long-deserted corners of the cathedral brought to light some interesting and curious relics of past days. In the eastern crypt are a number of slight incisions in the walls, most prominent on the west wall where Christ sits in the midst of the Four Evangelists; on the north side this seems to have been paralleled by an almost invisible coronation of Our Lady. On a pillar is the somewhat sinister apparition known as Becket's Ghost, probably nothing more than the remains of the coal so long piled against the walls and pillars there. More controversial was the discovery of a skeleton under the floor, a few feet from where the tomb of Becket had once stood. This gave rise to the supposition that his bones might have been extracted from the shrine before its destruction in 1538 and reinterred near their former resting place. This theory is now discredited in the light of modern scientific examination.

The lovely Chapel of St Anselm was restored in 1882 at the expense and initiative of Canon F. J. Holland, a well-known Victorian divine and residentiary canon of the cathedral. He wished it to be used again for private prayer and early celebrations, and was eventually buried there under a memorial brass. A painted reredos was set up, and in 1886 Prior Oxenden's great Decorated window was filled with glass by Clayton and Bell. (Both reredos and glass were destroyed in the blitz of 1942.) But the most precious of all the discoveries of this period was the mural painting of St Paul and the Viper which appeared when an internal buttress was removed to be replaced by an external one. Since this chapel was originally dedicated to St Peter and St Paul, there was doubtless a similar painting of some event in the life of St Peter. It would have been painted when artists were at work on Prior Conrad's choir and St Gabriel's Chapel in the early twelfth century. When the internal buttress was put up on the north side of the apse it certainly hid the painting, but it also protected it for posterity.

An account of the funeral of Dean Payne-Smith in 1895 shows that dignity and ceremonial had begun to return to the cathedral services.

The old customs were observed. The Dean was carried in through the west door (all others of the Chapter through the north-west door) and laid on a violet covered bier in the midst of the nave. The choir and canons on either side. My bedesmen had their white staves tied with black ribbon.

The writer was Dr E. W. Benson who succeeded Dr Tait as archbishop in 1883, and filled the Chair of St Augustine with great dignity until 1896. He is shown in the great window of the chapter house, restored soon after his death, very handsome and venerable with white hair, presiding over the Lambeth Conference of 1888. That year Canon Rawlinson gave a jewelled cross for the High Altar and two brass standard candlesticks. An elaborate Gothic screen was placed behind the altar to separate it from the area of the Trinity Chapel, but this disappeared soon after the First World War.

Benson was the last primate to live at Addington and the first to be buried in the cathedral since Cardinal Pole. His enthronement was attended by a huge congregation wearing, according to his son and biographer A. C. Benson, 'the lily of the valley, supposed emblem of Thomas à Becket'. The archbishop took a great interest in the doings of his cathedral church and was not always happy about the way the chapter conducted their business. In 1892 he wrote: 'We have no notion of how to use our cathedrals ... chapels, aisles, ambulatory, nave ... all are nothing to us and yet we are satisfied with ourselves.' The opening of the tomb of Hubert Walter and the placing of the ornaments discovered there in the cathedral library evoked from him the disgusted comment:

To his sons and brothers in the most sacred part of the church the Archbishop commended himself for ever and had laid with him the loveliest symbols of his earthly work. They, breaking all honour, reverence, and grace plunder him. They wonder people are bent on breaking up cathedrals and think little of their worship.

In another letter he records how he had always refused to look at the things taken out of the tomb.

84

His interest in the cathedral and its life is shown by his gift to the chapter of a sum of money which, invested, would provide a sum for the travelling expenses of the honorary canons of one guinea when they came to preach the annual sermon on Sunday afternoons. (His request that two furnished rooms should also be provided so that they could spend a week there at the same time is no longer remembered or honoured.) When he died he was laid under the north-west tower and a cenotaph was erected with his effigy on it. His real memorial, however, is not in stone but in the widespread use all over the Christian world of the service of Nine Lessons and Carols which he devised for Truro Cathedral when he was Bishop there, basing it on medieval liturgical precedents. He lived just half a century too soon. Within thirty years of his death the great renaissance of Canterbury Cathedral and many other great churches had begun, and the whole building had come to life and light again.

14

The Twentieth Century and the Exhilarating Renaissance

Benson's successor Frederick Temple was a link between two eras. His place in English history would have been summarized neatly in the words proposed for his cenotaph : 'Born under the Fourth George he crowned and blessed the Seventh Edward.' But the dean (Wace) ruled out any mention of George IV, so the inscription now to be seen is : 'He lived through the reigns of William IV and Victoria and crowned Edward VII.' The monument in the Corona is a very fine one in Cornish granite with an imposing kneeling figure of the archbishop in bronze.

During his primacy Addington Palace was sold and with the money thus made available the Old Palace of Canterbury was restored. Mr Caroe, the architect, retained much of the old house, and added new wings, a chapel, and a lecture room, and finished it off with a small turret. Here from time to time floats the flag with the heraldic shield of the see, the pallium of the archbishop and the primatial cross on a blue ground, indicating that the archbishop is in residence. With a charming and manageable house nearby the ties binding archbishop and cathedral have grown stronger and more affectionate since he is able now to take part in cathedral services in addition to those on high festivals.

Temple's colleague in the deanery was the celebrated novelist F. W. Farrar.[1] In eight years as dean he was responsible for raising £20,000, a great sum at that time, for restoration. The chapter house was completely restored, its large east and west windows filled with glass by the firm of Hemming. In the east window are great figures in Canterbury history, and in the west window incidents in which

---

[1] Familiar to Victorian readers as the author of the schoolboy novels *Eric or Little by Little* and *St Winifred's or the World of School.*

86

they participated. The reopening of this hall, which gave the city and diocese a superb meeting place, was the occasion of the first royal visit for many years. George IV had been to the cathedral in 1798 while still Prince of Wales, but although Queen Victoria had visited Canterbury she had not taken the trouble to visit the cathedral. Now, in 1897, Edward Prince of Wales and his much loved wife Alexandra were to be seen in the chapter house. The rejoicings were great and the city was *en fête* for the occasion. The splendours of the restored building with its gilded roof and medieval heraldry which now included the coats of arms of all the primates from Lanfranc to Frederick Temple must have impressed the royal couple. A new century and a new reign had begun when Temple died and was laid to rest in the Cloister Garth, to be followed by Dean Farrar the following year.

The next archbishop, Randall Thomas Davidson, was to preside over diocese and province for a quarter of a century, including the terrible years of the First World War. He was no stranger to Canterbury, for he had been chaplain to Archbishop Tait, whose daughter he had married, as well as a six preacher, although he had relinquished this office on his appointment as Dean of Windsor. The new dean, Henry Wace, was to be in office for twenty years. During this period the great event in the history of the cathedral was the raising of some £27,000 with which Bell Harry was completely repaired as well as the west or Twin Towers.

The tomb of Archbishop Henry Chichele, one of the finest in the cathedral, had been restored in 1897. The restoration was carried out by All Souls College, Oxford, which he had founded, and had involved new statues, heraldry, and much repainting. And in 1903 a large window was inserted in the west wall of the south-west transept in memory of Mr O. Waterfield. Designed and executed by Christopher Whall, it has three main divisions in the pre-Raphaelite style, showing the Nativity of Christ at the bottom, the Agony in the Garden in the middle, and the Resurrection at the top. Each scene is placed between single figures of saints, and the whole brilliant effect, owing much to the use of white glass and rich colouring, is in striking contrast to Austin and Caldwell's attempts to recreate thirteenth-century glass.

The years leading up to the First World War saw the cathedral established in the firm pattern of Anglican life with ample manpower and a sound liturgical tradition. Dean Wace was a solid and rather conservative evangelical churchman, presiding over a chapter of sound scholars and able men who all had distinguished careers in the Church before accepting their residentiary canonries. There were at this time still six residentiaries and usually four minor canons headed by the precentor and sacrist. On the lay side there were six vergers led by the senior and junior vesturers, and twelve bedesmen, with a musical staff of organist and deputy organist, a choir school of day boys only, and some half dozen lay clerks.

Services were numerous and followed strictly the order of the Book of Common Prayer. They were conducted with solemn dignity: when the archbishop came to service he was met by the dean and escorted in, preceded by two vergers with maces and his chaplain with cross. The Daily Offices were announced by the summons of Bell Harry when a verger with mace would call at the deanery to escort the dean. On Sundays the King's Scholars in surplices would be waiting to bow low to him on his way to service in the choir. Right down to the Second World War six of the bells in the south-west tower would be chimed half an hour before service on Sundays; three were chimed on weekdays. In 1913, while a student at the Jesuit College in Canterbury, Teilhard de Chardin attended Evensong at the cathedral, listened to the grave Anglican chants, admired the choristers in their violet cassocks and broad white collars, and noted the 'très gentleman canon'.

But this was still the day of locked gates and closed chapels in English cathedrals, and if the young Jesuit had sought to penetrate the deep recesses of the crypt or examine the tombs in the Trinity Chapel, he would only have done so with a verger in attendance after paying a fee. This was partly due to an error of judgement on the part of the Victorian clergy who had refused the offer of the Ecclesiastical Commissioners to take over such farms and estates as were left to them after the reforms early in Victoria's reign. (The Commissioners would have produced enough money to maintain the fabric and pay the clerical and lay staff.) When the value of rents and tithes fell at the end of the nineteenth century a financial crisis ensued and the canons residentiary had to forgo part of their incomes to enable other servants of the Church to be paid. The exaction of fees to see the building can only have helped slightly to alleviate the situation.

Yet the cathedral was waking to new life under the impact of the new century and the new reign. Organ recitals, gatherings of free-

88

masons, friendly societies, and diocesan associations became more frequent. Great national events like the death of Edward VII and the coronation of George V were observed with special services which drew vast congregations. Dr Charlton Palmer, who was the organist for the first thirty-five years of the century, and a devoted church musician, was a friend of Sir Edward Elgar. This friendship resulted in the greatest musical event in the cathedral's history up to that time, when in 1914 Elgar himself conducted a special performance of *The Apostles*. Two hundred players of the New Symphony Orchestra and six eminent soloists sat on a platform erected under the west window of the nave for this memorable occasion.

Despite the drain of manpower during the First World War, the daily services of the cathedral continued undisturbed, and on 11 November 1918, Mattins and Evensong were sung as usual with a full setting of the canticles and anthem as they had been throughout those terrible years. During that time there had been many special services of intercession, and in 1916 one Sunday was set apart with penitential litanies and sermons. This was a result of the call to penitence and humiliation made by the archbishops in face of the horrifying casualties of the war. Also in 1916 Archbishop Davidson led a procession of witness through Canterbury in which all the city churches joined. He presided too at the service held annually on 4 August to commemorate the outbreak of the war. Every Sunday morning throughout the war there was a vast parade of soldiers in the nave, and to solve the problem of acoustics a huge velarium, or awning, was suspended. It was in use, also, for the great gathering of all the clergy of the diocese from 11 January to 14 January 1916, under the presidency of the archbishop.

When peace returned there were innumerable requests to put up individual tablets and regimental memorials. The old chapter bowling green was transformed into the Kent War Memorial: a lovely garden with a great cross in the centre. A war memorial reredos to the men of the Buffs Regiment was erected in the Warriors' Chapel of St Michael, and a book with the names of the fallen was placed there on a lectern made by Mr Bainbridge Reynolds. Ever since, it has been the custom for a soldier from the Buffs Regiment at 11 a.m. each day to turn a page of this book, which holds several thousand names and was written and illustrated by Mr Graily Hewitt. (In June 1934 the bell of HMS *Canterbury* was presented to the cathedral and since then six bells have been struck as a prelude to the daily ceremony.) The ancient glass was replaced in the windows of the cathedral, and the elaborate screen behind the High Altar was removed. Visitors' fees began to flow in again, reaching £1,580 in 1919. The choir and the nave could be seen without payment, but vergers collected a fee of sixpence for showing parties round the rest of the building. (They themselves received five per cent of the total fees collected during the year.) At that time the cathedral organist was paid £250 per annum with a free house in the precincts, the senior vesturer £250 without a house, and the headmaster of the Choir School £240, from which was deducted £12 10s for his house on which he paid the rates. To heat the cathedral with anthracite cost just under £364 a year.

Dean Wace died in 1924 and his successor was Dr Bell, who had been domestic chaplain to Archbishop Davidson. It was an inspired appointment, for the new dean had a wealth of ideas about religion and art, poetry, and music, and above all how to use cathedrals more effectively in the life of the Church in the twentieth century. Though he was dean for only five years before becoming Bishop of Chichester, he managed to revolutionize the cathedral and drag it firmly out of the Victorian era in which it still lingered right into the post-war world with all its opportunities. Admission charges were abolished and the voluntary offerings that poured in soon far exceeded the money formerly received in fees. Chapels long deserted and empty of furniture were equipped with altars and brought back to use. These included the Deans' Chapel off the Martyrdom, St Martin's Chapel in the north-east transept, which was furnished as a memorial to Viscount Milner, and the little chapel of St Augustine under the north-west tower in which Archbishop Benson had been buried and which became a memorial to his friend Canon A. J. Mason.

A temporary altar was set up at the east end of the nave which was much used for services on summer evenings and big festival occasions. The high vaults of the nave and choir were equipped with new electric lighting. Regular meetings of the greater chapter of honorary canons were instituted as the dean wished to get as much support as possible from the clergy of the diocese. A great diocesan pilgrimage took place in 1925 in which a procession representing all the parishes of the diocese filed past Archbishop Davidson as he stood by the Marble Chair in the Corona. The long morning service on Sundays was considerably shortened, the sung Litany and

Ante Communion disappeared, and on the last Sunday of each month a Choral Communion took the place of Mattins.

A silver crucifix with a gilt figure of Our Lord was dedicated for processional use. Special festivals were held to mark the seven-hundredth anniversary of the first Franciscans in Canterbury in 1224, and the tercentenary of the death in Canterbury of the great composer Orlando Gibbons in 1625. The BBC was invited to relay a sung service from the cathedral, and ecumenical activities were not neglected when a memorial service was held for Cardinal Mercier whose palace in Malines had been the scene of the famous Conversations not long before Bell's arrival in Canterbury.

The dean's artistic interests found vigorous expression in the first Canterbury Festival of Music and Drama in 1927. Holst conducted *The Planets*, *Everyman* was performed outside the West Front of the cathedral and *Dr Faustus* in the chapter house. The Friends of the Cathedral was formed that year, and in 1928 they held their first Festival and announced their first restoration project. This was to be the lovely Norman water tower of Prior Wibert which had long been an ivy-clad and dilapidated structure. In 1928 also the first 'mystery play' to be performed in a cathedral in England since the Reformation was produced in the nave. Written by Masefield, it was a Nativity play called *The Coming of Christ*, and it drew vast crowds. Holst wrote the music for choir, organ, piano, and solo trumpet, and Charles Reckitts designed the costumes. Performed entirely by local people, the whole production caused a great sensation.

A few weeks later Archbishop Davidson announced his resignation, the first primate to resign in the history of the Church of England. The enthronement of his successor, Dr Cosmo Gordon Lang, was the most magnificent ceremony the cathedral had witnessed since the end of the Middle Ages. Superbly produced by the dean and his canons, it was undoubtedly a great ecclesiastical and national occasion in which procession and pageantry, fine music, and dignified ceremonial combined to create an act of worship which was to set a standard for subsequent enthronements. Dr Bell took endless pains to ensure that the traditional ceremonial of the installations had a sound historical basis. The day chosen was 4 December 1928, the anniversary of the consecration of St Anselm in 1093, and the Marble Chair was placed for the first time at the head of the steps leading from nave to pulpitum. There the dean, following the precedent of medieval priors, enthroned the new primate before a vast concourse of people. This was followed by the singing of a Te Deum written for the occasion by Dr Vaughan Williams, in which the choir of the Chapel Royal joined the cathedral choir. At the end of the service the new archbishop gave a blessing to the city and the people from a special platform erected in front of the west doors.

In 1929 Dr Bell was appointed Bishop of Chichester.

At his consecration in Canterbury Cathedral Archbishop Lang wore a cope, and in spite of protests it was not long before the dean and canons wore them on festival occasions. The archbishop also began to wear a mitre, and at festival services in the cathedral servers wore albs and tunicles, and banners and lights were carried in the processions.

The new dean was Dr Sheppard, famous for his broadcasts as vicar of St Martin's in the Fields. The universal pleasure at his appointment was sadly spoilt by his ill-health. Fearful attacks of asthma proved too much for him and he resigned in 1931. When fit and well he attracted vast crowds to the cathedral services, and he presided at the funeral of Archbishop Davidson in 1930. He had also been present at the opening service of the Lambeth Conference at which there was a great Orthodox delegation headed by the Patriarch of Alexandria. When Dr Sheppard died in 1937 he was buried near Archbishop Davidson in the Cloister Garth. And in the west alley of the cloisters is a charming window by Hugh Easton in memory of him, in which he is seen kneeling as a shepherd worshipping the Christ Child in the manger at Bethlehem.

PART IV

The Cathedral in the Modern Age

15

The Second World War:
Prelude and Aftermath

In 1931 Dr Hewlett Johnson was installed as dean, and for the next thirty-two years the Church of England was to hear much of Canterbury and its celebrated 'Red Dean'. Up to the outbreak of war there were many notable changes in the cathedral, mainly for the better. The dean himself made a great contribution towards the enrichment of the services and the ceremonial, while the Friends of the Cathedral carried out, in association with the dean and chapter, many additions and improvements to the fabric and furnishings.

After the restoration of the Norman water tower and the first Friends' Festival, Miss Margaret Babington became steward and treasurer of the Friends. Her ability to attract people into the fellowship of the Friends and to persuade them to make gifts of money for their projects, or to give things of beauty to the cathedral, was truly remarkable. Every year the annual Friends' Festival in midsummer attracted more people. For at this stage Canterbury was a pioneer again in matters artistic and cultural, as it had so often been in the past. People flocked to hear the BBC orchestra play great music in the nave, or to hear serenades in the cloisters. They came also to enjoy religious plays written specially for Canterbury by eminent writers. T. S. Eliot's *Murder in the Cathedral* was first performed in the chapter house. Dorothy Sayers' plays, *The Zeal of Thine House* and *The Devil to Pay* were almost as exciting to watch as Eliot's great drama of St Thomas.

Professor Tristram was at work on the restoration of the mural paintings in the crypt chapels and St Anselm's Chapel, as well as the restoration and reconstruction of the painted testers and headboards of the royal tombs of the Black Prince and Henry IV. Many of the other famous tombs began to glow with colour again under his skilful direction as the dirt and dust of ages was cleaned off. Most astonishing of all was the Black Prince's effigy which, after cleaning, turned out to be a glorious gold colour. Professor Tristram was responsible also for the handsome wrought-iron stand for the primatial cross in the nave as well as a banner for the Friends. Medieval colour and glory was restored to the Christ Church Gate. The turrets demolished early in the nineteenth century were rebuilt, and the shields on the south façade were recoloured, making this one of Canterbury's most splendid sights.

Among the many improvements carried out by the Friends before the war was the levelling of the Cloister Garth. Over the years it had risen in height and had been filled with graves and memorial stones so that the level was several feet above the cloister walk. Tons of earth were carted away and unimportant tombstones removed, leaving only those of Archbishops Frederick Temple and Randall Davidson, and Deans Wace and Sheppard. When this work was in progress, a tenth-century Saxon pocket sundial was found embedded in the earth. It resembled the Mass dials so often found in the lintels of ancient churches into which a pin was inserted to show the time of Mass. The little pocket sundial was devised for a similar purpose and must have belonged to someone of wealth or importance since it is made of silver with a gold cap and chain. As a relic of Saxon times it is one of the greatest treasures of the cathedral.

An interesting addition at this time to the larger ornaments of the cathedral was a replica of a fifteenth-century statue of St Thomas of Canterbury, in full pontificals, given by the Church in Sweden. It has been placed in the Norman crypt, one part of the cathedral which would still be familiar to St Thomas. The nave was also enriched by the gift of the Great Stalls, finely carved in wood to seat twenty people. Magnificent iron grilles behind them closed in the area of the nave in the bay next to the sanctuary round the altar of the Holy Cross. Together with the Bodley pulpit and the new altar, they gave much dignity and beauty to the east end of the nave.

The quality of the music and the ordering of the services improved greatly and made Canterbury a model cathedral in the conduct of public worship. This was partly the result of the reorganization of the Choir School. In 1937 it became a boarding school in a charming house in the Brick Walk in which was incorporated the fourteenth-century Table Hall of the monastic infirmary. The headmaster, the Revd Clive Pare, the organist, Mr Gerald Knight, and the

Precentor, the Revd Joseph Poole, together built up a very high standard of worship in the cathedral.

In 1935 Dr Shirley became headmaster of the King's School and was faced with saving it from disaster and bankruptcy. He persuaded his colleagues on the chapter to advance a considerable capital sum in order to enlarge and improve the accommodation, and to allow him to turn some of the houses formerly occupied by cathedral clergy into boarding houses and a dining hall. In a very short time the number of boys at the school increased, and they gave impressive dramatic performances in the chapter house and fine orchestral and choral concerts in the cathedral. They also set a high standard in those cathedral services for which the school was responsible.

The Munich crisis of 1938 alarmed the chapter sufficiently for them to order the great twelfth-century genealogical figures to be taken out of the south-west transept window. This turned out to be a dress rehearsal for the events of September 1939. The medieval treasures of glass and the monuments of archbishops and royal princes were protected until 1945 by sandbags, corrugated iron, and concrete enclosures built round them. The exterior leaded roof was painted green and earth was brought into the choir ambulatories, while the crypt became an air-raid shelter. The organ had been dismantled in 1939 to be rebuilt by Messrs Henry Willis, but their works in Brixton were demolished by a bomb and much of the organ was destroyed. (The restored organ and its new console did not appear in the cathedral again until 1948, and until then a Hammond organ was used.)

In 1941, under the terms of the Cathedrals' Measure of 1931 and 1934, the Cathedrals' Commission revised the statutes of the cathedral for the first time since the days of Alford. Few changes were made when the revised statutes were published in 1942. By this stage in history, the number of stalls for residentiary canons had been reduced to four and the number of stipendiary as opposed to honorary minor canons to two: the precentor and the sacrist. On the other hand, the number of honorary canons had risen in less than a century to something like twenty-four; there still remained unchanged the six preachers, and twelve bedesmen on the Foundation, though there have seldom been more than four or five bedesmen in modern times.

Archbishop Cosmo Lang resigned in 1942. He had loved Canterbury and in his fourteen years there had seen much that was

97

exciting happen to the cathedral, though his relations with his dean over the last few years had often been anything but cordial. If he was the last of the Victorian archbishops by training and in outlook, his successor William Temple was very much a man of the modern age. The son of Archbishop Frederick Temple, he knew Canterbury well, and his enthronement was a magnificent affair in a crowded cathedral and a city as yet almost unaffected by enemy action.

Only six weeks later, on a brilliant moonlit night, Canterbury was bombed and by morning half of the old city within the walls had vanished for ever. Thanks to a wonderful team of fireguards who patrolled the roofs night after night during the war, the cathedral escaped unscathed, the incendiary bombs being dealt with promptly and effectively. Only the cathedral library had a direct hit from a high explosive and was a complete ruin, though most of the books were salvaged. Some of the houses on the south side of the precincts had been destroyed, and the King's School dining hall was gutted and roofless. Despite all this savage destruction the cathedral services continued without a break, a choir of seventeen day boys under the direction of Precentor Poole amazingly maintaining their high standards. (The boarders at the Choir School had been evacuated to Cornwall in 1940 where they remained with the headmaster until 1945.)

In the early summer of 1944 there were three great services in the nave for the men of the Allied Forces who were to take part in the invasion of Europe. Soon after, the flying bombs began to fall over Kent and southern England, but the cathedral passed unscathed also through this fearful period of the war.

On 18 September, as the gliders were flying over the cathedral on their way to the great battles around Arnhem and Nijmegen, Archbishop William Temple assembled all the clergy of the diocese in the choir to talk to them about the tasks which would face the Church of England after the war, and how they could best be tackled. To the deep concern of all, the archbishop had to be carried in to address his clergy. He was clearly a very sick man, but still the news of his death on 26 October fell like a thunderbolt on the whole Christian community in England and across the world. A vast congregation of people genuinely mourning a great leader filled the cathedral from end to end at his funeral. His ashes were laid in the Cloister Garth near his father's tomb, and in due course the chapel of St John the Evangelist was furnished as his memorial to a design by Stephen Dykes Bower.

On the Feast of St Alphege, 19 April 1945, Geoffrey Fisher was enthroned as Temple's successor. For the first time the historic Anglo-Saxon Gospels sent over by Pope Gregory the Great to St Augustine c. 600 were used at an enthronement. Representatives of Corpus Christi College, Cambridge, which had owned them since the time of Archbishop Parker, offered them to the Archbishop to touch when he made his corporal oath.

Then began the work of reconstruction. Dr Fisher set himself to put in order the Church's finances and to modernize its canon law. Dean Johnson and his canons arranged for the rebuilding of the bombed houses in the precincts. Ancient glass was put back into the windows, and tombs and monuments emerged from their protective covering. On 8 May, VE Day, a vast crowd of more than a thousand people had poured into the nave spontaneously for an impromptu service of thanksgiving. On 20 October there was a formal Thanksgiving Service for the return of the King's School from its wartime evacuation. The Lesson was read by Field-Marshal Montgomery who had spent a short time at the school when his grandfather, F. W. Farrar, was dean.

The following summer King George VI attended a great service of Thanksgiving for the preservation of the cathedral. Afterwards he presented the King's School with a new Royal Charter, thus commemorating the Letters Patent of 1541 which had established the school as part of the cathedral foundation. He also unveiled five shields in the north alley of the cloister which had been blazoned with his own arms and those of his Queen, Queen Mary, Princess Elizabeth, and Princess Margaret. (Frank Salisbury painted a large picture of the occasion which hangs in the north choir aisle.)

16

Restoration, Recovery, and the Primacy of the Hundredth Archbishop

The restoration of the cathedral to something of its true splendour was made possible by an appeal which raised £260,000. The American banker, Mr Thomas Lamont, donated half a million dollars which was used, among other things, to install a completely new oil-fired heating system, the old one having been destroyed in the bombing of 1942. Under the skilful direction of Professor Tristram the nave pulpit was discreetly coloured, and Cardinal Kemp's tomb was given back some of its medieval glow and richness. The vanished picture of the Annunciation on Cardinal Morton's tomb was repainted around the pot of lilies which was all that had survived Puritan attacks and the decay of centuries.

The Friends' Festivals were restarted in 1946 and distinguished authors, including Christopher Fry, wrote new plays around such Canterbury figures as St Alphege and Stephen Langton. Among lovely things given to the cathedral after the war, none was more lovely than a seventeenth-century Portuguese ivory statue of Our Lady. It was placed in the niche over the Altar of Our Lady Undercroft where a tall solid silver statue had stood in the Middle Ages. Window by window the ancient glass went back. (The Friends published a splendid volume by Bernard Rackham illustrating and describing it.)

New windows by contemporary artists replaced some of the nineteenth-century glass of Austin and Caldwell which had been destroyed in 1942. These included a fine heraldic window by William Wilson showing the arms of the Colonels of the Buffs which was placed in the east window of the Buffs Chapel of St Michael. A rather disappointing window commemorating the coronation of Queen Elizabeth II was placed over the Martyrdom door. It was executed by the firm of Comper and given by the Freemasons of Kent. Four windows by the Hungarian artist Ervin Bossanyi were inserted in the south-east transept and have been much admired. Many think that the St Anselm window, the work of Harry Stammers, placed in that saint's chapel, is one of the most colourful and exciting of the modern windows.

The organ, restored and enlarged by Henry Willis, was opened in 1949. Although the pipes went back to their old place in the triforium, the console was resited on the great stone pulpitum. The Revd Joseph Poole had left Canterbury, after maintaining musical standards so valiantly during the war, and Gerald Knight continued as organist and Master of the Choristers until 1952. The Royal School of Church Music, later installed at Addington Palace, was then in one of the houses in the Brick Walk, and all through this period the music in the cathedral continued to be of a high quality. Special services and oratorios by the King's School and the Canterbury Choral Society made the cathedral a great centre of musical activity. All the time the number of visitors was increasing, and participating in special festivals such as that organized by the city and the cathedral together as part of the Festival of Britain (1951).

All through history the cathedral had been recognized as one of the great masterpieces of medieval art and architecture. Now the famous and important began to be seen coming through Christ Church Gate again as Henry VIII and Charles V had come more than four centuries before. Amongst the most notable visitors have been Mahatma Gandhi, the Venerable Patriarch of Moscow, the Ecumenical Patriarch from Istanbul, and Mr Bulganin, Mr Kruschev, and Mr Malenkov. Since the Second Vatican Council many distinguished Roman Catholics have appeared officially at cathedral services, and Cardinal Suenens, Archbishop of Malines-Brussels, preached at Evensong one Sunday in 1974.

The appearance of the precincts began to change as new buildings went up. A new library, designed by John Denman, was opened in 1954 on the site of the old bombed library, the west wall of Lanfranc's dormitory being retained in it. On the far side of the Howley-Harrison Library, an additional library was built on the ruins of the old monastic Chequer Building. It was designed by Harold Anderson and made possible by a generous gift from the Wolfson Foundation.

Inside the cathedral, many monuments as well as marble pillars and pavings were cleaned and repaired. After the surcoat and armour of the Black Prince had been restored, these were placed in a special case at the foot of the Pilgrim Steps, modern copies made by the armourers of the Tower of London being set over the tomb. The Warriors' Chapel, damaged by bombing, was also restored. Two large pictures were bought from the Cook collection. A large St Christopher by the sixteenth-century Italian artist Garofalo now hangs on a pillar at the west end of the nave, and a lovely Adoration of the Shepherds by Bartolomeo Schidoni is behind the altar of St John the Evangelist in the south-east transept.

The King's School took over Meister Omers and the adjoining house as boarding houses as well as the east end of the house known as Chillenden Chambers. Occupied traditionally by the archdeacon of Canterbury, it had been wrecked by a bomb in 1940, but was rebuilt as the Larder Gate of the old monastery. Above all, in 1957, a neo-Tudor Great Hall was built for the school between the Old Palace and the main school buildings capable of seating more than a thousand people, and named the Shirley Hall after the headmaster.

Gifts continued to pour in for the adornment of the cathedral. A lovely Calvary altarpiece in Australian bean wood and aluminium designed by Andar Meszaros was given for St Anselm's Chapel; and a handsome new door-case for the south-west corner of the nave in which was used some of the carving of the choir seats made two and a half centuries before. In recent years some more of this handsome panelling has been utilized in the west crypt to screen off electrical fittings and other necessary but unsightly installations.

In 1948 and again in 1958 the Lambeth Conference opened once again with a great service in the cathedral, the archbishop sitting in 1958 in the Chair of St Augustine on the steps in front of the Screen of the Six Kings to welcome the hundreds of bishops from all over the Anglican Communion. At the Friends' Festival that year Sir Adrian Boult made his last appearance conducting the BBC Orchestra. And a few weeks afterwards Margaret Babington died. Steward and treasurer of the Friends for so many years, she was over eighty and had been planning a world tour to raise money for their work. Her ashes were laid to rest in a corner of the Cloister Garth, and her family coat of arms was set up on the vault above. The great and costly work of refacing the thirty-two bays of the cloisters was already in progress, and one was restored as the memorial of the children of the diocese to Margaret Babington.

The enormous task of repairing the stonework of Bell Harry was begun in 1963. Ten years' work was set in hand on the great tower which disappeared under a web of scaffolding. Archbishop Fisher resigned in 1961, and was succeeded by Dr Michael Ramsey. The cathedral had never looked more splendid than at his enthronement, its glass back again and the tombs and monuments cleaned and restored. It was the last great occasion on which Hewlett Johnson was to appear as dean. He retired in 1963 and was succeeded by Ian White-Thomson. The new dean's father had been Archdeacon of Canterbury, and later Bishop of Ely, and he himself had been domestic chaplain to Archbishops Lang, Temple, and Fisher.

In 1961 Dr Sydney Campbell, the cathedral organist, went to Windsor and was succeeded by Allan Wicks, and in 1962 Dr Shirley resigned as headmaster of the King's School to devote himself to the work of his canonry. In the years after the war the two apsidal chapels in the crypt dedicated to St Nicholas and St Mary Magdalene had been restored by Canon Shirley and Canon Julian Bickersteth respectively. In these chapels their ashes were laid to rest when they died.

Maundy Thursday 1965 was an unforgettable occasion when for the first time the Royal Maundy was distributed in the cathedral. The Queen was attended by the Lord High Almoner and the Yeomen of the Guard, and the traditional leather purses were distributed to old men and women from all over the diocese.

In 1970 a whole year of festival was held to commemorate the eight-hundredth anniversary of the martyrdom of St Thomas of Canterbury. The cathedral was brilliantly relit, and floodlit outside as well. The Archbishops of Sens and Rheims took part in a special service and the former unveiled a tablet in the cloisters to commemorate the exile of St Thomas in Sens, and also William of Sens. Many concerts and plays were given in the cathedral, including a three-week run of Eliot's *Murder in the Cathedral*. A *Son et Lumière* production was given in the Green Court, and the year ended with a solemn commemoration of the Martyrdom on the day itself, 29 December. A winter flower festival began in the Martyrdom and was arranged all the way down the north side of the Norman undercroft and into the great central space of the east crypt where the tomb of the Martyr had stood until 1220. After the Festival Year was over it was decided to commemorate the burial in the Trinity Chapel Shrine with an inscription in brass let into the floor. This inscription now reads: 'The shrine of Thomas Becket Archbishop and Martyr stood here from 1220 to 1538.' In addition, a carved statue of Christ by W. Day, a local artist, depicted as welcoming the pilgrim and visitor, was placed just inside the south-west porch.

The Becket Festival was the logical culmination of the great festivals of the Friends. These are now usually confined to two days, one for youth and one as a gathering for the Friends. Instead, the King's School have long mounted their own festival known as King's Week, and since 1970 the Summer Arts Festival has been largely based on the cathedral and its musical events.

Gradually over the years a veritable army of stewards, caterers, guides, and chaplains has been assembled to cope with the vast number of visitors from many parts of the world. A company called Cathedral Gifts Ltd has been formed by the chapter to look after the whole business of publications which modern tourism seems to need and demand.

In 1972 the Choir School was reorganized and today some thirty boys grouped in the Choir House are linked with St Edmund's School for educational purposes. They still live in the old house in the Brick Walk, sing the daily services and travel up and down to school in a mini-bus. The thirty boys and the twelve lay clerks maintain a very high standard of singing, with a large repertoire ranging from the ancient Advent antiphons and other plainsong chants to settings and anthems by contemporary composers. Mattins is no longer sung on weekdays, but Evensong continues to be sung daily and, since 1973, the Eucharist in the Series 3 rite has become the usual Sunday morning service.

In 1974 a week of festival was held to commemorate the 750th anniversary of the coming of the Franciscan Friars to Canterbury in 1224. The Roman Catholic Franciscan Fr Agnellus Andrew preached at the closing service in the nave at which representatives of the Anglican Society of St Francis and the Roman Catholic Orders were present. Seven weeks later Archbishop Ramsey resigned, and before the year was out the dean and the canons, residentiary and honorary, had elected as their archbishop Dr Donald Coggan, Archbishop of York. Five days later he launched an appeal for his cathedral church for £3,500,000. The three objects of the appeal were the complete restoration of the crumbling stonework of the fabric, restoration of the ancient stained glass eaten away by atmospheric pollution, and the securing of a suitable sum for endowing the historic musical foundation of the cathedral.

17

Epilogue 1975:
The Magnificent Enthronement

Dr Donald Coggan was enthroned on the Eve of the Feast of the Conversion of St Paul in the Week of Prayer for Christian Unity. The congregation was one of the largest and most representative ever assembled in the British Isles, a tribute to the great surge forward of the Ecumenical Movement during the primacy of Archbishop Ramsey. Among all the representatives of the Free Churches of England and the Orthodox Churches of the East were to be seen the apostolic delegate representing the Vatican, and three cardinals in scarlet birettas. This sight would have astonished even those present at the translation of St Thomas just over 750 years before.

When everyone had been blessed in choir and nave and outside the cathedral, when the last fanfares had died away, the last sounds of organ and choir gave way to the tumultuous ringing of bells. Then the traditional promises of obedience were made to the archbishop, in the majestic gloom of the chapter house, by all those on the Foundation of the cathedral, assembled before the Prior's Seat. The enthronement ended in the west crypt where the great ones of Church and State took off their robes and ate and drank the refreshments provided for them among the famous Romanesque carvings and under Ernulf's vault. If the shades of those who had known and loved this place in past centuries, St Anselm and St Thomas, Erasmus and the Black Prince, and the twentieth-century primates who had lain in state here before their funerals in the church above, were in any way present, they must have looked with wonder but also with loving approval at so unusual a spectacle within the walls of Christ's glorious church in Canterbury.

Appendices

Index

APPENDIX
1

The Archbishops of Canterbury

1 St Augustine 597
2 St Laurentius 604
3 St Mellitus 619
4 St Justus 624
5 St Honorius 627
6 St Deusdedit 655
7 St Theodore of Tarsus 668
8 Berchtwald 693
9 St Tatwine 731
10 Nothelm 735
11 Cuthbert 741
12 St Breogwine 759
13 Jaenberht 766
14 Aethelhard 793
15 Wulfred 805
16 Feologild 832
17 Ceolnoth 833
18 Aethelred 870
19 Plegmund 890
20 Athelm 914
21 Wulfhelm 923
22 St Odo 942
23 St Dunstan 960
24 Ethelgar 988
25 Sigeric 990
26 Aelfric 995
27 Aelfeah (Alphege) 1005
28 Lyfing 1013
29 Aethelnoth 1020
30 Eadsige 1038
31 Robert of Jumièges 1051
32 Stigand (deprived 1070) 1052
33 Lanfranc 1070
34 St Anselm 1093
35 Ralph D'Escures 1114

36 William de Corbeuil 1123
37 Theobald 1139
38 St Thomas Becket 1162
39 Richard 1174
40 Baldwin 1185*
41 Reginald FitzJocelyn 1193
42 Hubert Walter 1193
43 Stephen Langton 1207
44 Richard Grant 1229
45 St Edmund Rich 1234
46 Boniface 1245
47 Robert Kilwardby 1273
48 John Peckham 1279
49 Robert Winchelsey 1294
50 Walter Reynolds 1313
51 Simon Mepham 1328
52 John Stratford 1333
53 John Ufford 1349
54 Thomas Bradwardine 1349
55 Simon Islip 1349
56 Simon Langham 1366
57 William Whittlesey 1368
58 Simon Sudbury 1375
59 William Courtenay 1381
60 Thomas Arundel 1397
61 Roger Walden 1398
   Thomas Arundel restored 1399
62 Henry Chichele 1414
63 John Stafford 1443
64 John Kemp 1452
65 Thomas Bourchier 1454
66 John Morton 1486
67 Henry Dean 1501
68 William Warham 1503
69 Thomas Cranmer 1533

70 Reginald Pole 1556	84 Thomas Herring 1747
71 Matthew Parker 1559	85 Matthew Hutton 1757
72 Edmund Grindal 1576	86 Thomas Secker 1758
73 John Whitgift 1583	87 Frederick Cornwallis 1768
74 Richard Bancroft 1604	88 John Moore 1783
75 George Abbot 1611	89 Charles Manners-Sutton 1805
76 William Laud 1633	90 William Howley 1828
(vacancy after Laud's	91 John Bird Sumner 1848
execution in 1645	92 Charles Thomas Longley 1862
until 1660)	93 Archibald Campbell Tait 1868
77 William Juxon 1660	94 Edward White Benson 1883
78 Gilbert Sheldon 1663	95 Frederick Temple 1897
79 William Sancroft 1678	96 Randall Thomas Davidson 1903
(deprived 1690)	97 Cosmo Gordon Lang 1928
80 John Tillotson 1691	98 William Temple 1942
81 Thomas Tenison 1695	99 Geoffrey Francis Fisher 1945
82 William Wake 1716	100 Arthur Michael Ramsey 1961
83 John Potter 1737	101 Frederick Donald Coggan 1974

* The exact number of archbishops is controversial. Some authorities omit Reginald FitzJocelyn who was elected in 1185 but died before consecration; and also John Ufford, a similar case ... elected in 1349 but dying of the Black Death before consecration, thus making 99 to the present day (1975). And some count Thomas Arundel twice over, since he was deprived by Richard II and then restored by Henry IV, but this seems rather absurd. I prefer the figure 101.

APPENDIX
2

Deans and Priors of the Cathedral

DEANS

Cuba 798	Maurice I 930
Beornhead 805	Aelfwyn 930
Heahfrith 813	Alsine 935
Ceolnoth 820	Aelfwyn II 951
Aegelwyn 830	Athelsinc*
Eadmund 871	Aegelnoth 984
Alfric*	Egelfric 1026
Kensyn*	Goderic 1058

PRIORS

Henry 1080	Nicholas de Sandwich 1244
Ernulf 1096	Roger de St Alphege 1258
Conrad 1114	Adam de Chillenden 1264
Gosfrid 1126	Thomas Ringmere 1274
Elmer 1128	Henry de Eastry 1285
Jeremy 1137	Richard Oxenden 1331
Walter Durdens 1143	Robert Hathbrand 1338
Walter Parvus 1149	Richard Gillingham 1370
Wibert 1153	Stephen Mongeham 1376
Odo 1167	John Fynch 1377
Benedict 1175	Thomas Chillenden 1391
Harlewine 1177	John Wodensburgh 1411
Alanus 1179	William Molash 1428
Honorius 1186	John Salisbury 1438
Roger Norris 1189	John Elham 1446
Osbern de Bristow 1190	Thomas Goldstone I 1449
Geoffrey 1191	John Oxney 1468
Walter III c.1213	William Petham 1471
John de Sittingbourne 1222	William Sellinge 1472
John de Chatham 1232	Thomas Goldstone II 1495
Roger de Lee 1234	Thomas Goldwell 1517

* Exact date unknown

DEANS
THE NEW FOUNDATION

Nicholas Wotton 1542
Thomas Godwyn 1567
Richard Rogers 1584
Thomas Nevil 1597
Charles Fotherby 1615
John Boys 1619
Isaac Bargrave 1625
George Aglionby 1642
Thomas Turner 1643
John Tillotson 1672
John Sharp 1689
George Hooper 1691
George Stanhope 1704
Elias Sydall 1728
John Lynch 1734
William Friend 1760
John Potter 1766
Hon Brownlow North 1770
John Moore 1771

Hon James Cornwallis 1775
George Horne 1781
William Buller 1790
Folliott Herbert Walker Cornwall 1793
Thomas Powys 1797
Gerrard Andrewes 1809
Hon Hugh Percy 1825
Hon Richard Bagot 1825
William Rowe Lyall 1845
Henry Alford 1857
Robert Payne-Smith 1871
Frederick William Farrar 1895
Henry Wace 1903
George Kennedy Allen Bell 1924
Hugh Richard Lawrie Sheppard 1929
Hewlett Johnson 1931
Ian Hugh White-Thomson 1963

Index